Israeli-Palestinian Conflict

David Robson

LUCENT BOOKS

A part of Gale, Cengage Learning

GALE
CENGAGE Learning™

Detroit • New York • San Francisco • New Haven, Conn • Waterville, Maine • London

GALE
CENGAGE Learning™

LIBRARY OF CONGRESS CATALOGING-IN-PUBLICATION DATA

Robson, David, 1966–
  Israeli-Palestinian Conflict / by David Robson.
    p. cm. -- (World history)
  Includes bibliographical references and index.
  ISBN 978-1-4205-0239-8 (hardcover)
  1. Arab-Israeli conflict--Juvenile literature. 2. Jewish-Arab relations--Juvenile literature. I. Title.
  DS119.76.R63 2010
  956.04--dc22

                                        2009040746

Lucent Books
27500 Drake Rd.
Farmington Hills, MI 48331

ISBN-13: 978-1-4205-0239-8
ISBN-10: 1-4205-0239-5

Printed in the United States of America
  2 3 4 5 6 7 14 13 12 11 10

Printed by Bang Printing, Brainerd, MN, 2ⁿᵈ Ptg., 12/2010

Contents

Foreword

Each year, on the first day of school, nearly every history teacher faces the task of explaining why his or her students should study history. Many reasons have been given. One is that lessons exist in the past from which contemporary society can benefit and learn. Another is that exploration of the past allows us to see the origins of our customs, ideas, and institutions. Concepts such as democracy, ethnic conflict, or even things as trivial as fashion or mores, have historical roots.

Reasons such as these impress few students, however. If anything, these explanations seem remote and dull to young minds. Yet history is anything but dull. And therein lies what is perhaps the most compelling reason for studying history: History is filled with great stories. The classic themes of literature and drama—love and sacrifice, hatred and revenge, injustice and betrayal, adversity and overcoming adversity—fill the pages of history books, feeding the imagination as well as any of the great works of fiction do.

The story of the Children's Crusade, for example, is one of the most tragic in history. In 1212 Crusader fever hit Europe. A call went out from the pope that all good Christians should journey to Jerusalem to drive out the hated Muslims and return the city to Christian control. Heeding the call, thousands of children made the journey. Parents bravely allowed many children to go, and entire communities were inspired by the faith of these small Crusaders. Unfortunately, many boarded ships captained by slave traders, who enthusiastically sold the children into slavery as soon as they arrived at their destination. Thousands died from disease, exposure, and starvation on the long march across Europe to the Mediterranean Sea. Others perished at sea.

Another story, from a modern and more familiar place, offers a soul-wrenching view of personal humiliation but also the ability to rise above it. Hatsuye Egami was one of 110,000 Japanese Americans sent to internment camps during World War II. "Since yesterday we Japanese have ceased to be human beings," he wrote in his diary. "We are numbers. We are no longer Egamis, but the number 23324. A tag with that number is on every trunk, suitcase and bag. Tags, also, on our breasts." Despite such dehumanizing treatment, most internees worked hard to control their bitterness. They created workable communities inside the camps and demonstrated again and again their loyalty as Americans.

These are but two of the many stories from history that can be found in the pages of the Lucent Books World History series. All World History titles rely on sound research and verifiable evidence, and all give students a clear sense of time, place, and chronology through maps and timelines as well as text.

All titles include a wide range of authoritative perspectives that demonstrate the complexity of historical interpretation and sharpen the reader's critical thinking skills. Formally documented quotations and annotated bibliographies enable students to locate and evaluate sources, often instantaneously via the Internet, and serve as valuable tools for further research and debate.

Finally, Lucent's World History titles present rousing good stories, featuring vivid primary source quotations drawn from unique, sometimes obscure sources such as diaries, public records, and contemporary chronicles. In this way, the voices of participants and witnesses as well as important biographers and historians bring the study of history to life. As we are caught up in the lives of others, we are reminded that we too are characters in the ongoing human saga, and we are better prepared for our own roles.

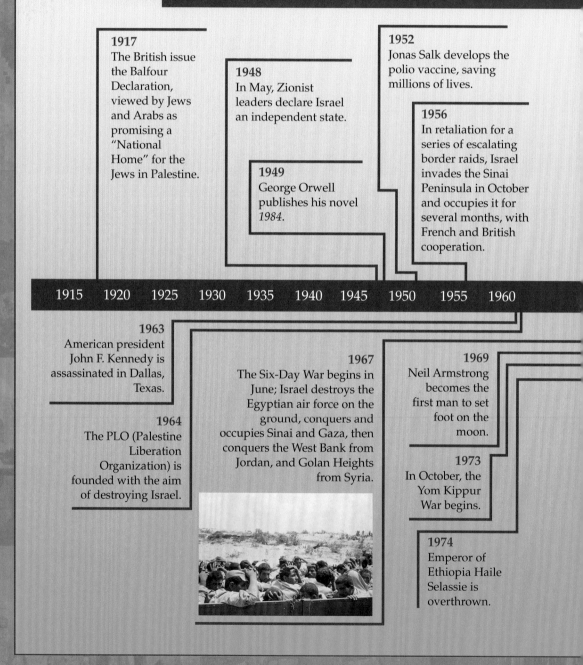

1917
The British issue the Balfour Declaration, viewed by Jews and Arabs as promising a "National Home" for the Jews in Palestine.

1948
In May, Zionist leaders declare Israel an independent state.

1949
George Orwell publishes his novel *1984*.

1952
Jonas Salk develops the polio vaccine, saving millions of lives.

1956
In retaliation for a series of escalating border raids, Israel invades the Sinai Peninsula in October and occupies it for several months, with French and British cooperation.

1915   1920   1925   1930   1935   1940   1945   1950   1955   1960

1963
American president John F. Kennedy is assassinated in Dallas, Texas.

1964
The PLO (Palestine Liberation Organization) is founded with the aim of destroying Israel.

1967
The Six-Day War begins in June; Israel destroys the Egyptian air force on the ground, conquers and occupies Sinai and Gaza, then conquers the West Bank from Jordan, and Golan Heights from Syria.

1969
Neil Armstrong becomes the first man to set foot on the moon.

1973
In October, the Yom Kippur War begins.

1974
Emperor of Ethiopia Haile Selassie is overthrown.

of the Israeli-Palestinian Conflict

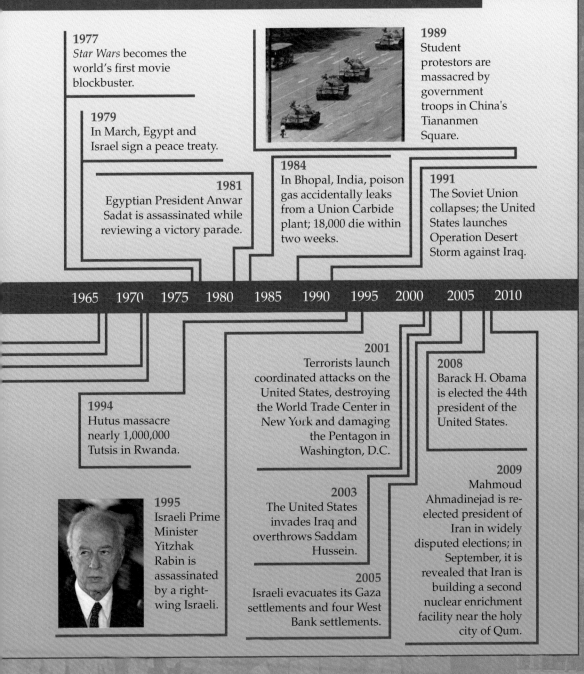

1977
Star Wars becomes the world's first movie blockbuster.

1979
In March, Egypt and Israel sign a peace treaty.

1981
Egyptian President Anwar Sadat is assassinated while reviewing a victory parade.

1984
In Bhopal, India, poison gas accidentally leaks from a Union Carbide plant; 18,000 die within two weeks.

1989
Student protestors are massacred by government troops in China's Tiananmen Square.

1991
The Soviet Union collapses; the United States launches Operation Desert Storm against Iraq.

1965   1970   1975   1980   1985   1990   1995   2000   2005   2010

1994
Hutus massacre nearly 1,000,000 Tutsis in Rwanda.

1995
Israeli Prime Minister Yitzhak Rabin is assassinated by a right-wing Israeli.

2001
Terrorists launch coordinated attacks on the United States, destroying the World Trade Center in New York and damaging the Pentagon in Washington, D.C.

2003
The United States invades Iraq and overthrows Saddam Hussein.

2005
Israeli evacuates its Gaza settlements and four West Bank settlements.

2008
Barack H. Obama is elected the 44th president of the United States.

2009
Mahmoud Ahmadinejad is re-elected president of Iran in widely disputed elections; in September, it is revealed that Iran is building a second nuclear enrichment facility near the holy city of Qum.

Decades of Conflict

For decades Jewish Israelis and Arab Palestinians have fought over an area the size of the state of New Jersey. Each believes that the land rightfully belongs to them, and each is willing to fight to control it. The conflict has killed thousands, injured countless more, and sewn such seeds of hatred that lasting peace remains elusive.

The path to peace may run through typical Israeli settler Sharon Katz's hilltop suburb called Efrat and the other seventeen Jewish settlements in the West Bank. Home to nearly 300,000 people, the settlements are patrolled around the clock by Israeli soldiers because beyond the settlement walls is a population of 2.5 million Palestinians who believe the West Bank is rightfully theirs and that the Israelis must leave.

Katz has no intention of leaving. She and her husband, Israel, moved to the West Bank in 1985 from Woodmere,

New York, and are certain that Israelis have a divine, God-given right to the disputed territory won by Israel in the Six-Day War of 1967. "We are living in the biblical heartland,"[1] she says. She refuses to acknowledge any Palestinian claim to the land, believing the Arabs did not move into the area until the 1970s. "Jews started coming here and to talk of a community. That's when the Arabs started coming here."[2]

One of those Arabs is Naim Sarras, a middle-aged farmer, and he can see Efrat from his small farm. He disputes Katz's view of history and says his family has maintained the land for 150 years. He grows grapes and olives but makes little money and accuses Israelis of poisoning his olive trees. "I am willing to live with Israelis," says Sarras, "But they will not live with us."[3]

Neither Sarras nor Katz sees much cause for hope in the ongoing dispute between Israelis and Palestinians. Both refuse to cede land to an age-old enemy; both claim a long-standing right to live where they live, regardless of the consequences.

Background to the Issue

The Israeli-Palestinian conflict is a battle over land. It pits the State of Israel, established in 1948, against a community of Arabs, known as Palestinians, living in the area. Both peoples claim ancient rights to the disputed terrain. But in modern times, open disagreement and religious differences have led to war, destruction, and the killing of thousands of people.

Because Israel was a nation originally carved out and manufactured by a European mandate, it has always been deemed illegitimate by its Arab neighbors in the region. A series of wars followed in which the Israelis captured lands not initially part of their modern boundaries. But fearing more external threats, they retained the land for security purposes and because many Israelis believed it was part of their destiny as a people.

The Palestinians, meanwhile, believe that at least a portion of that disputed land, now called the Occupied Territories, belongs to them. Exhaustive attempts at finding a peaceful resolution have found mixed success, sometimes leading to formal treaties and the trading of land for peace. At other times

Israeli tanks enter Jerusalem during the Six-Day War in 1967.

potential diplomatic breakthroughs have only led to mutual resentment and continued violence.

Why Is It Important?

Because the Israeli-Palestinian conflict continues to defy solution, many observers believe it will never change. Nearly every day, newspapers around the world carry stories of the latest negotiations or the latest reports of casualties in Ramallah or Tel Aviv. The lives of average Jewish Israelis and Palestinians hang in the balance as their politicians wage verbal warfare and fight for the diplomatic upper hand.

The Israeli-Palestinian conflict sits at the center of a geographic storm—the Middle East—where the conflict has often stoked heated debate and revealed long-held anti-Semitism, or hatred of Jewish people. For the international community, solving the conflict is an essential part of stabilizing the Middle East as a whole, since developed nations depend on Middle Eastern crude oil, which can be refined into gasoline, to fuel their societies. This dependence puts countries, including the United States, Great Britain, China, and Japan, at the economic mercy of Arab nations and organizations that tightly control the valuable resource and also sympathize with the plight of Palestinians. Nations both friendly and hostile to Western interests agree that unless the Israeli-Palestinian conflict is solved the region has little hope of finding peace in the twenty-first century.

For people of faith, the conflict is more personal and painful. Many of the most sacred sites for Muslims, Jews, and Christians are located in Israel and the Occupied Territories. Known collectively as the Holy Land, the area is home to some of humankind's oldest religious traditions. Ongoing war in the region only promises to cause more friction between people of different religious backgrounds.

What Can It Teach Us?

Few conflicts have been as long, bitter, or bloody as the one between Israelis and Palestinians. Over the years, both sides have worked to gain strategic victory, often to the detriment of their own best interests and those of their people. Militarily superior to its Palestinian foes, Israel regularly uses its might to crush any resistance to its occupation of territory populated primarily by Palestinians. This occupation is considered illegal by the United Nations, a world body comprised of hundreds of member nations. Conversely, militant Palestinians have often used terrorism to frighten Israelis and force them to give in to demands for a Palestinian state. Death and destruction have only fed the animosity each group feels for the other. After more than sixty years, the conflict provides a stark reminder of the limits of diplomacy. When warring sides are unwilling to set aside past differences and violence to find common ground, any hope for lasting peace remains unlikely.

Chapter One

Origins of the Conflict

Centuries of war have made the Middle East what it is today, changing its landscape and its people. The State of Israel, surrounded by the countries of Egypt in the west, Lebanon and Syria in the north, and Jordan in the east, is a tiny place—300 miles (483km) long and 40 miles (64.4km) wide; still, it may be the most bitterly contested land in human history. But during the first half of the nineteenth century, the region, then known as Palestine, appeared to be a forgotten and forsaken place.

Ottoman Rule

For five hundred years the Ottoman Empire in Turkey ruled Palestine yet cared little for its welfare or its people. American writer Mark Twain visited the area in 1867 and provides an outsider's perspective: "Of all the lands there are for dismal scenery, I think Palestine must be the prince. . . . It is a hopeless, dreary, heart-broken land."[4]

Most of the people living in Palestine's towns and on its farms were Arabs of Muslim faith, and they disliked the empire's growing relationship with Europe. Centuries before, Christian crusaders from Europe invaded the Holy Land. They captured Jerusalem and slaughtered thousands of innocent Arabs. Arabs, therefore, remained suspicious of European intentions in the Middle East. They also distrusted Palestine's Ottoman commander, Ibrahim Pasha, and when Pasha began drafting the Arabs into the Turkish army, Arab citizens of Palestine rioted.

Although Pasha and his forces violently put down the rebellion, the Arabs had united behind a common cause for the first time. The uprising encouraged them to identify themselves as Arabs, not as citizens of the Islamic Ottoman Empire. This newfound unity and sense of identity only increased, but the Arabs of Palestine were also forced to cope with a growing influx of vocal Jews who were now actively calling for a Jewish homeland.

Jewish Diaspora

Palestine was already home to small Jewish enclaves, although most Jews fled the area after centuries of persecution at the hands of Romans, Christians, and Turks. By the late 1800s, Jewish communities dotted the world. Many in this Jewish diaspora, or dispersal, were content in their exile. In Europe, especially, Jews thrived. They were able to maintain their unique traditions by living in communities separate from other Europeans. Orthodox Jews, who practiced a devout form of Judaism, also dressed differently and abided by strict dietary rules. They excelled in business, in some cases earning great wealth through money lending. But Jewish accomplishment came at a price: Europeans expected Jews to fit in to their societies and abandon their ancient heritage.

Jewish leaders and thinkers began openly discussing what it meant to be Jewish and how best to integrate their traditions and beliefs into European so-

Devout Jews gather and read scripture at the holy Wailing Wall in Jerusalem.

ciety. An intellectual and cultural "Enlightenment," *haskala*, grew among educated Jews who often changed their family names to make them sound more European or abandoned their cultural and religious customs to appear less Jewish.

But all was not well. European anti-Semitism did not disappear; instead, it grew.

Often, Jews were made scapegoats and targeted by governments and ordinary citizens in deadly hate crimes, or pogroms. Christians routinely blamed Jews for the death of Jesus Christ and stereotyped them as greedy and dishonest, with hook noses, sharp teeth, and strange religious practices. The view of Saint John Chrysostom, an early Christian writer, is typical: "Shall I tell you of their plundering . . . their abandonment of the poor, their thefts, their cheating in trade?"[5] These kinds of distortions and lies convinced some Jewish thinkers that a radical plan of action was needed to ensure the long-term survival of the Jews.

Moses (middle, wearing white robe) reveals the God-given tablets containing the Ten Commandments to the people of Israel.

Zionism

The concept of Zionism grew from the belief among some Jewish intellectuals that other nations would never accept them completely; they needed their own, independent nation in the land of their forefathers to protect themselves and a set of unique beliefs more than three thousand years old. The foundation of Judaism is a belief in the covenant, or agreement, between God and Abraham in which God promised to bless Abraham's descendants. Subsequently, God's laws—the Ten Commandments—were revealed to the prophet Moses and given to the Jewish people. In time, the early Jews built a nation, the kingdom of Israel. The term "Zionism" derives from an ancient term for this kingdom, also known as Zion.

Israelites and Canaanites

According to legend, the Jewish people evolved in the Land of Canaan thousands of years ago. Abraham's Promised Land passed to his grandson, Jacob, but a terrible famine forced Jacob, also known by the name Israel, and his family to flee and eventually settle in Egypt.

Once they arrived, Jacob was forced into slavery. His descendants remained enslaved until Moses, a Jewish prophet, led the Jews out of Egypt and into the desert. There, God had Moses transcribe the Ten Commandments onto large tablets. These laws of faith would become the foundation of Judaism. By 1200 B.C. the Jews arrived in the Land of Canaan. But they were not alone. Nomadic tribes of Canaanites or Philistines also made a home here and were unwilling to part with it. The arriving Jews gave them little choice, subduing them through warfare and eventually founding the kingdom of Israel in 1050 B.C.E. (Before Common Era). As time went on, the Israelites acquired even more land, including what became the city of Jerusalem. In 930 B.C.E., the kingdom fell on hard times and split into two nations, Israel and Judah. Resulting wars led to the destruction of the great temple and the deportation of thousands of Jews.

The first Zionist colony in Palestine was founded by Russian Jews in 1882. Another group, Hovevei Zion (or Lovers of Zion), gave interested Jews money and helped them get into Palestine secretly. By most accounts, the early Zionist settlers were poorly organized but united in their distrust for the Arabs surrounding them. Jewish community leader Moshe Smilansky wrote that separation was essential: Jews must "keep their distance from the fellahin [Arab farmers] and their base attitudes . . . lest our children adopt their ways and learn from their ugly deeds."[6]

Determined as they were to build a Jewish state, the early Zionists had no consistent voice until a Hungarian Jew named Theodor Herzl became involved in the movement. Herzl had studied to be a doctor but found his calling as a writer. Although he was well aware of the widespread persecution of Jews in Europe, it was the infamous Dreyfus Affair that first inspired Herzl's Zionist zeal. In 1894 a French official discovered papers in a trash can that suggested a military officer was passing state secrets to Germany. French army captain Alfred Dreyfus, a Jew, was immediately accused of the crime despite little evidence of his guilt.

Before the trial even began, right-wing activists took to the streets chant-

Famed Zionist Theodor Herzl poses alongside his three children in his office.

ing "Down with the Jews"[7] and calling for Dreyfus's conviction. During the secret military court-martial that followed, Dreyfus pleaded innocent, but the trial's outcome was little more than a foregone conclusion. Dreyfus was convicted of treason, stripped of his military rank, and sent to Devil's Island in South America as punishment.

Herzl followed the newspaper accounts of the Dreyfus Affair and was horrified. An educated, assimilated Jew like himself had been falsely convicted of a crime simply because he was Jewish. According to historian Benny Morris, "Herzl reached a dismal conclusion: There was no hope and no future for the Jews in Europe."[8] Without a separate and independent Jewish state, Herzl believed the Jews of Europe would eventually be destroyed; mass emigration to another land was their only chance for survival.

In 1896 Herzl published *The Jewish State*, a political pamphlet in which he argues his case for a Jewish homeland: "We have honestly endeavored everywhere to merge ourselves in the social life of surrounding communities and to preserve the faith of our father. We are not permitted to do so. . . . Let all who are willing to join us, fall in behind our banner and fight for our cause with voice and pen and deed."[9]

Written in simple, clear language, Herzl's call resonated with thousands of Jews across the continent. A year later, Herzl organized the First Zionist Congress in Basel, Switzerland. With more than two hundred in attendance, the congress designed a framework to make the dream of founding a Jewish state in Palestine a reality.

Herzl soon approached European leaders to ask for their help, even offering Sultan Abdulhamid II of Turkey billions of dollars, which Herzl did not have, for any land the sultan was willing to part with. The Sultan rejected the idea and the money. Equally unsuccessful was Herzl's attempt to bargain with wealthy European Jews. To them, Herzl's plan seemed unrealistic; they also feared appearing disloyal to their adopted nations. Despite these disappointments, Herzl's vision caught on with the broader Jewish population: By 1900 twenty-one Zionist settlements existed in Palestine with as many as fifty thousand Jews living in them.

At times, the Jewish community of Palestine, or Yishuv, tried to purchase land from Arabs willing to sell. If this failed, they staked claims for unfarmed or unwanted tracts of land. But life for the settlers could be harsh and unforgiving as they tried to farm an unfamiliar land and acclimate themselves to their new surroundings. Some gave up the dream after a few months and returned to Europe or emigrated to the United States. Those who stayed were more determined than ever to forge a Jewish state in the land of their biblical forefathers. But their fate was not yet in their own hands.

British Rule

In 1914 the armies of Germany and Austria battled those of Great Britain,

France, Russia, and the United States in a conflict that became known as World War I. The Ottoman Empire joined the side of Germany and Austria. But the empire was too poor and too weak to be of much help in the fighting.

As the war raged on, vocal Zionist groups convinced the British to aid them in founding a Jewish homeland in Palestine if Germany, Austria, and the Ottoman Empire were defeated. The resulting Balfour Declaration was drafted in 1917 and promised a Jewish state in Palestine. It did not specify exactly how much of the land the Jews would be given. For Foreign Secretary Arthur Balfour, such details hardly mattered. The needs of the Jews trumped any Arab claim on the land: "Zionism right or wrong, good or bad, is rooted in age-long traditions," he said, "and in present needs and future hopes of far profounder import than the desires of 700,000 Arabs."[10]

While the Balfour Declaration was making news in Europe, British forces, aided by Arab rebels, moved into the Arabian Peninsula and took control of

Britain's Lord Arthur Balfour (middle, wearing sunglasses) visits Jerusalem in 1925, following the formalization of the controversial Balfour Declaration.

Syria and Palestine. The Ottoman Empire was no more. After World War I ended in 1919, a variety of Arab tribes laid claim to what is now Saudi Arabia. Great Britain and France took much of the rest, dividing the areas into so-called mandates that were designed to exist only until the inhabitants could rule themselves. In reality, the two European nations essentially created colonies that they alone controlled; they installed Arab governments with British and French interests in mind.

Having promised the Jews a homeland, the British installed no Arab leaders in the mandate of Palestine. Instead, they agreed to control the region themselves. In the meantime, the Arabs of Palestine began to unify around their resistance to British rule. They feared that the British would officially adopt the Balfour Declaration and that the Jews would take their land. At about this time, they also began referring to themselves as Palestinians and claiming an ancient and unique history that they believed gave them the right to call Palestine their home.

When the League of Nations, an international governing organization, formalized the Palestine Mandate in July 1922, they included the Balfour Declaration. The document's preamble states its primary purpose: "Whereas

The Rise of Islam

By A.D. 600 Arab populations living in the southeast portion of Palestine consisted of nomadic warriors, known as bedouins, as well as those who lived in small towns and villages. Despite an ethnic similarity, Arab tribes rarely got along peacefully. But in 610 Muhammad, Islam's founder and prophet, began preaching the word of Allah, meaning "The God," across the Arabian Peninsula. Muhammad spoke of receiving revelations from God, and his companions thereafter memorized and recorded these revelations, known as the Koran, or Qur'an. Muhammad's message of submission to one, all-powerful God resonated deeply with many Arabs, and he was able to unite his converts and attack the weakened empires of Persia and Rome. In little more than a century, Muslims conquered all of what is known today as the Middle East as well as portions of Spain and North Africa. They took Palestina from the Romans in A.D. 637. They began referring to Palestina by the Arabic "Filastin," and Arabic became the official language. Jerusalem became Al Quds, or "City of the Holy," and the Arabs built a new mosque, a Muslim religious shrine. Called al Masjid al Aqsa, the mosque was located at one end of the Temple Mount, a sacred place for both Jews and Muslims.

the Principal Allied Powers have also agreed that the Mandatory should be responsible for putting into effect the declaration . . . in favor of the establishment in Palestine of a national home for the Jewish people, it being clearly understood that nothing should be done which might prejudice the civil and religious rights of existing non-Jewish communities in Palestine."[11]

Despite the declaration's stated intentions to recognize the rights of non-Jews, the Palestinians rejected it. The British, they believed, favored the Jews. If they did nothing, their land would be stolen and they would never get it back. The complicated nature of the region— peopled by those of differing faiths and distinct ideas about who had a legitimate claim on the land—made governing a challenge for the British. Their hopes of influencing the people of Palestine with their Christian values and political ideas failed dramatically. To ensure their influence, the Zionists meanwhile created the Jewish Agency, which coordinated immigration efforts with the British government. Their willingness to work with and please Great Britain paid dividends: By 1924 another influx of Jews had entered the Holy Land. The new arrivals quickly got to work trying to buy land, but Palestinians no longer sold them any. Regardless, the Zionists began large construction projects, building roads and permanent structures like museums and houses. One of the labor unions doing the work—the Histadrut—was led by a young Polish Jew named David Ben-Gurion.

Ben-Gurion and other Zionist leaders tried to ignore Arab resistance to their presence and went about creating new lives in a place they hoped would one day be a legitimate nation. For protection against Palestinian violence, the Zionists also organized a small militia, the Haganah. For cultural legitimacy, the Zionists lobbied the British to make Hebrew an official language in Palestine. Meanwhile, Palestinian and British negotiations over land broke down. Attempts to dispose of or change the Balfour Declaration failed; in frustration, Palestinian militias lashed out at Jewish settlers, often killing them. But the Jews fought back, having smuggled arms into Palestine for years. By the 1930s, though, Palestinian groups had become more violent and the British permitted the Haganah to fight back. Eventually, Palestinian resistance was crushed. "The Palestinians entered the fighting . . . with a deeply divided leadership, exceedingly limited finances . . . and no reliable allies," writes historian Rashid Khalidi. "They faced a Jewish society in Palestine which . . . was politically unified."[12]

World War II and the Holocaust

In the early 1930s in Germany, Chancellor Adolf Hitler unified his own Nazi Party, promising to return his country to its former glory. An essential element of that resurgence was anti-Semitism, which Hitler and his underlings actively promoted in their speeches and party literature. After Hitler was elected

Jewish museum visitors view gruesome photographs of Nazi death camps. Approximately six million Jews were killed in the Holocaust.

chancellor in 1933, the Nazis passed race laws, severely curtailing the human rights of German Jews and laying the groundwork for an all-out assault on European Jewry as a whole.

As Hitler's armies gobbled up Austria and Poland and headed toward the Soviet Union in the East, Nazis and their collaborators began the mass killing of Jews. What began informally in small towns in Eastern Europe soon became a formalized attempt to murder all the Jews in Europe. Nazi concentration and death camps began executing Jews and others they deemed undesirable on a massive scale. By the war's end in 1945, the Aryan nation had killed 6 million Jews and 6 to 8 million others in what became known as the Holocaust.

More than ever, the world's Jewish population required a homeland where they could protect themselves from destruction. But in Palestine, the British refused to allow more Jews to relocate to the Holy Land. They feared the new arrivals would only agitate the Palestinians even more. Instead, the prohibition on Jewish immigration turned many in the Zionist movement away from their former allies. If the British refused to give them the homeland they felt they had earned, they would fight for it.

One early Zionist settler made it clear: "The Ultimate goal . . . is, in time, to take over the Land of Israel and to restore to the Jews the political independence they have been deprived of for these two thousand years. . . . The Jews will yet arise and, arms in hands (if need be), declare that they are the masters of their ancient homeland."[13]

British Withdrawal and Partition

When the British again balked at allowing more Jews into Palestine, Ben-Gurion ordered the Haganah to attack. "Ben-Gurion wanted to fight . . . and forge a Jewish nation," says historian Martin Gilbert. "His vision of a democratic Jewish state and his strategy for attaining it shaped the fight of the new Israelis against their enemies."[14]

On October 1, 1945, Zionists destroyed a Palestinian railway and held mass demonstrations. Less than a year later, Irgun, an offshoot of Haganah, planted bombs at a Jerusalem hotel, site of the British Army headquarters. The goal was to frighten the British and force them to give in to Zionist demands for increased immigration. The resulting explosion murdered ninety-one people and weakened British resolve in the region.

Irgun's actions notwithstanding, many people around the world supported the idea of a Jewish state. An American public opinion poll taken in December 1945 showed that 76 percent of Americans who followed events in Palestine were in favor of allowing Jews to live there. The Holocaust only made people more sympathetic to the plight of the Jews.

Great Britain had, by 1948, lost sympathy for both sides of the conflict and was looking desperately for a way out of Palestine. British representative to the United Nations Alexander Cadogan made his country's intentions known: "His Majesty's government have reached the conclusion that they are not able to bring about a settlement in Palestine based upon the consent of both Arabs and Jews. It is for this reason that they have brought the problem before the United Nations, hoping that the general assembly would be more successful in the search for an agreed settlement."[15]

Yet no country seemed to fully support a Jewish state, or was willing to say so. Then, in a surprise to all gathered at the United Nations headquarters in New York, Soviet delegate Andrei Gromyko spoke to the assembly saying, "We must recognize the elementary rights of the Jewish people to an independent sovereign state."[16]

Gromyko went on to propose a partition plan, which would divide the land in question into an Arab state and a Jewish state. Areas with a larger Arab population were to become part of the Arab state, including a large chunk of the Galilee in the north; Jewish areas, including the Negev in the south, would become part of the Jewish state. Jerusalem, near the center, was to become an internationally controlled city.

The UN Partition Plan, as it came to be known, was imperfect from the start. Its division of land favored the Zionists, awarding 55 percent of the land to the Jews, who previously owned only 7 percent. They accounted for 30 percent of Palestine's population. Much of the land given them was also located in the most fertile parts of the region. The Palestinians, on the other hand, were allotted 45 percent of the land, much of it arid and not fit to farm. The Jews appeared satisfied with this solution, but

David Ben-Gurion, the first prime minister of the Jewish state, led Israel in the fight for a democratic nation.

the Palestinians refused to accept a plan that accorded them less than half the land. The violence that followed proved they would not give up the fight easily.

In January 1948 Palestinian militias attacked, killed, and then mutilated the bodies of thirty-five Jewish troop reinforcements protecting a group of villages known as Gush-Etzion. "That was really very, very tough," remembers one Jewish fighter. "Listen, you kill your enemy, okay, why do you have to dismember him?"[17]

Such violence shocked the Jews and put them on notice for attacks not only against armed forces but against civilians, as well. "We were afraid that the fate of the thirty-five could be our fate, as well,"[18] says settler David Ben David.

Many northern cities contained both Arabs and Jews, and tensions were developing in these places too. The coastal city of Haifa remained under British control, and here the fading empire did all it could to slow the progress of Jewish immigration into Palestine. But their efforts proved futile. Their remaining forces retreated and left the Jews and Palestinians to find peace, if they could, on their own.

A sense of ownership persisted in both groups. Neither seemed likely to cave in to threats or acts of violence. Ben-Gurion, in his memoir, writes about Jewish rights and a responsibility to this ancient homeland: "We held a clear title to this country. Not the right to take it away from others (there were no others), but the right and the duty to fill its emptiness, restore life to its barrenness, to re-create a modern version of our ancient nation."[19]

Contrary to Ben-Gurion's claim, the Arabs already populated the desert land and claimed it as their own, and he knew it. This inconvenient truth may not have fit Ben-Gurion's vision, but the triumph and tragedy that followed would test the courage and determination of both Jews and Palestinians.

Chapter Two

Israel and Its Neighbors

As the Zionists of Palestine moved toward declaring a free and independent Jewish state in the Middle East, the Arab nations in the region worked harder than ever to defeat them. By supplying arms and man power to the people now known as the Palestinians, the Arabs signaled their refusal to accept the Jews. For the next three decades, the Middle East would often be consumed by all-out war as both sides battled for absolute supremacy.

First Arab-Israeli War

The Zionists were laboring to create a viable nation surrounded by Arab countries repelled by the notion of a Jewish state in the Middle East. Many Arabs viewed Zionism as a kind of racism—that Jews thought they were superior to Arabs and that Arabs' concerns were secondary. For years the European-backed rulers of Iraq, Jordan, Syria, and Lebanon refused to become directly involved. Now they decided they could no longer sit idly by as Zionists staked claims to Palestine.

In early 1948 the Arab League became directly involved in the brewing conflict. Formed in Cairo in 1945, the league's primary goals were to protect the independence and sovereignty of Arab nations. League members did not recognize Palestine as a legitimate and independent region. Historian Philip Hitti echoes the common Arab view of the time: "There is no such thing as Palestine in history,"[20] he says. Nor did Arab leaders consider Palestinians a distinct and separate Arab people. Instead, they wanted to divide all of Palestine among themselves. Subsequently, Arab League forces, made up of fighters from Egypt, Syria, Jordan, and Lebanon, joined the Palestinians in a last ditch effort to defeat the Zionists. Attacks and counterattacks followed into April.

On April 10 Jewish forces attacked Deir Yassin, a Palestinian village, and killed 120 people. Palestinians responded by ambushing Irgun as they withdrew their wounded fighters. The intense fighting forced thousands of Palestinians to flee their homes, their neighborhoods, and even entire cities. Certain they could one day return, they packed all of their belongings and ran for their lives.

The Jewish settlers were fighting for their own lives and now took bold action. The British intended to withdraw their last troops from Palestine by August 1, 1948, but on May 14, 1948, Ben-Gurion and fellow Zionists appeared at the Tel Aviv Museum to officially declare Israel an independent, democratic nation: "By virtue of our natural and historic right and on the strength of the resolution of the United Nations General Assembly . . . we hereby declare the establishment of a Jewish state in Eretz [the land of] Israel, to be known as the State of Israel."[21]

Arab League soldiers in Jerusalem shoot at Jewish fighters during the First Arab-Israeli War.

The next day, Egypt, Syria, Lebanon, Jordan, and Iraq attacked Israel in what became known as the First Arab-Israeli War. The Israelis, though, were better armed than any of the five Arab nations. Their newly formed Israel Defense Forces (IDF) were well organized and prepared to face the Arab onslaught. Although they suffered hard losses—six thousand killed—the IDF also gained ground, taking portions of Palestinian territory. The fighting continued until November, when Arab armies quit the battlefield. Two months later, Egypt signed a cease-fire agreement with Israel. But the costs of war were high for the Arabs, particularly the Palestinians, who lost nearly sixteen thousand fighters and civilians. The Arab nations had gone into battle to conquer lands in Palestine that they wanted to control; the Palestinians, who now saw themselves as a separate and independent Arab people, had lost much more. Israelis held on to land promised them by the UN Partition Plan. But they now also controlled areas that the UN had promised the Palestinians, particularly in the northern and central parts of the region. The Arab nations, though defeated, also fared better than the Palestinians, taking charge of the territory included in the old mandate: King Abdullah of Jordan claimed the title king of Palestine and ownership of the West Bank and part of Jerusalem; Egypt took the Gaza Strip, along part of its eastern border.

Aftermath

Palestinians call this defeat "the Catastrophe" because it drove as many as one million of them into neighboring countries. Despite Palestinian pleas to the UN, Israel passed laws barring the return of these exiles. By the end of 1948, barely 150,000 Palestinians remained in the former Palestine, many of them separated from their families and left with little more than the clothes on their backs. They were "transformed into homeless refugees scattered around their lost country," writes historian Helena Lindholm Schulz, "while the small number who succeeded in clinging to their land were stripped of their property and of their most elementary human . . . rights."[22]

Although Israel gave the Arabs living in the territory Israeli citizenship in their new country, the Palestinian people would be forced to live under conditions dictated by the Israelis. In the years immediately following the First Arab-Israeli War, Palestinians residing in Israel were subject to martial law. This meant that they needed permits to travel outside the country, were forced to abide by strict curfews, and could be expelled from the country at any time. While they could do little to halt Israeli progress from within the Jewish state, militant factions of Palestinian refugees took up arms, determined to fight the Israelis to the death. These groups found financial and military support among Arab governments in Lebanon and Jordan and began making deadly raids into Israel. While these raids killed few Israelis, they gave the Palestinian commandos, or fedayeen, a sense of power that their daily lives lacked.

The Arab countries surrounding the new nation were also more determined than ever to oust the Jews. Arabs considered Israel stolen land and the actions of its Zionist leaders criminal. Still licking their wounds from the fractious war, they viewed the Israelis more as contemporary European crusaders than as an ancient people reclaiming a lost homeland. "The Jewish state had arisen at the heart of the Arab world," writes Morris, "and that world would not abide it . . . the man in the street, the intellectual in his perch, the soldier in his dugout—refused to recognize or accept what had come to pass."[23]

This refusal prompted the Arab League, the alliance of Arab countries, to call for an immediate boycott of trade with Israel. Although the policy was inconsistently enforced, the message was clear: Israel would not be recognized as a sovereign state.

The Rise of Nasser

Another Middle East power rose in 1952 when Gamal Abdel Nasser, a charismatic colonel, helped depose Egypt's king Farouk. Nasser became Egypt's second president in 1956 and inspired millions of Arabs by speaking out against European occupation in the Middle East. Fiercely anti-Israel and anti–Western influence, Nasser stoked nationalistic fervor within his own country but feared all-out war. "It would be utter madness," he said, "for Egypt to start a war with Israel on her own."[24]

Nasser was more concerned with ongoing British influence in the region, yet he remained a staunch enemy of the Jewish state. "He certainly regarded Israel as an unwelcome, alien presence in the region," writes Morris, "but respected its strength and probably feared its future intentions."[25]

Although fearful of taking Israel on directly, Nasser did allow Palestinian fighters to raid Israel from the Egyptian-controlled Gaza Strip. He also worked to better arm his nation by purchasing weapons from Czechoslovakia in Eastern Europe, a close ally of the Soviet Union. Tensions in the region came to a head in the fall of 1956 when the Eisenhower administration in Washington, D.C., fed up with Nasser's anti-Western views, scrapped plans to build a dam along the Nile River. With the support of the UN, Nasser responded to the U.S. action by taking control of the Suez Canal and ordering the British and French corporation running it to get out.

In response, the French, British, and Israelis devised a secret plan to invade Egypt and to oust Nasser. Code-named Operation Musketeer, the action commenced on October 29 when IDF tanks moved into the Gaza Strip and Sinai Peninsula. Quickly, their forces succeeded in routing the Egyptian army. Nasser's troops retreated but held off their attackers for a time by sinking their own ships in the canal as a way of stopping any further advance by British and French ships. The Western powers then bombed and destroyed nearly the entire fleet of Egyptian planes as they sat on the runway. They soon after took command of the canal.

Demonstrators in the Egyptian capital of Cairo protest British occupation of the Suez Canal.

Despite indirectly helping to cause the Suez War, as it came to be known, the United States had been careful not to publicly take sides during the conflict. Yet Eisenhower feared that if the fighting continued, the Soviet Union—the United States' fierce Cold War enemy—could step in and take Egypt's side; this would force the United States to become more directly involved militarily. Rising stakes could set off a third world war. As a way of avoiding such a confrontation, the U.S. government applied diplomatic pressure to Great Britain, France, and Israel to get them to withdraw their forces. The three nations eventually agreed to remove their troops from the Sinai Peninsula, but tensions remained high. "If a new status quo had been created," writes historian Michael B. Oren, "it was one of inherent instability, a situation so combustible that the slightest spark could ignite it."[26]

While the instability kept all key Middle East players on guard in the immediate aftermath of this second Israeli-Arab conflict, tempers cooled. Still, surrounded by nations hostile to its very existence, Israel did not back down and seemed willing, if necessary, to resume military action. "Our neighbors should not delude themselves that weakness prevents us from spilling blood,"[27] said Israel's third prime minister Levi Eshkol.

Israel was anything but weak, and its evolving ties with the United States only made it stronger. Eshkol became the first Israeli prime minister to officially visit the White House in June 1964. From the beginning, the United States had strongly supported the idea of a Jewish state, and more Jews lived in the United States than in any other nation in the world. American leaders like President Lyndon Johnson, therefore, recognized not only the moral rectitude of befriending Israel; they also understood the political importance of allying themselves with an influential bloc of voters. During Eshkol's visit to Washington that summer, Johnson gave Israel his country's complete backing: "The United States is foursquare behind Israel on all matters that affect their vital security interests."[28] Johnson also promised Israel $52 million in aid, with the stipulation that none of it be used to fund the Jewish nation's military. This way, Johnson could help the Israeli people but allay Arab fears that he was willing to support Israel in any future war.

Six-Day War

By 1966 the Israeli military needed all the help it could get. Israeli farmers in the northeast part of the country regularly farmed land that Syria said belonged to them. In retaliation, Syria cut off an important Israeli water supply from the Jordan River. Israeli cross-border gunfire led to shelling from the Syrians which led to Israel's shooting down of Syrian air force planes. Rumors of an Israeli invasion swept Syria in early 1967, but no Arab nations appeared willing to help the Syrian government protect itself.

Even Egypt's Nasser seemed reluctant, although the record suggests he felt confident in his country's ability to defend itself against Israeli forces. But eventually, the pressure to aid Syria and preserve his reputation as a powerful leader willing to confront Israel compelled Nasser to act: He ordered tanks into the Sinai Peninsula as he had years before and hoped for a different outcome. To guarantee a victory in any conflict with Israel, he also sent Egyptian ships to block an Israeli shipping lane to the vital Red Sea port of Eilat.

Then on May 16, 1967, government-controlled Radio Cairo announced a blunt threat: "The existence of Israel has continued too long. We welcome the Israeli aggression, we welcome the battle

Moshe Dayan

With his eye patch and bald head, Israeli defense minister Moshe Dayan cut an intriguing figure on the world stage. Born in 1915 on the Degania kibbutz, a Jewish settlement in Palestine, Dayan joined the Haganah at age fourteen and learned guerrilla tactics from a British captain. In 1939 the British outlawed the Haganah; Dayan was arrested along with hundreds of his colleagues in the force and imprisoned for two years. After being released, he joined the British army nonetheless and helped liberate Lebanon and Syria during World War II. It was during action in Lebanon that he lost his left eye. All the while, Dayan remained active in the Haganah and in 1948 commanded units defending Jewish settlements. By 1958 Dayan had entered the political arena, joining the Labor Party and being elected to the Knesset, or Israeli parliament, a year later. After serving as minister of agriculture for two prime ministers, Dayan was

Israeli military leader Moshe Dayan.

appointed defense minister shortly before the Six-Day War, for which he argued. Although the heavy losses in the Yom Kippur War forced his resignation, Dayan remained a force in Israeli politics until his death from cancer in 1981.

that we have long awaited. The great hour has come. The battle has come in which we shall destroy Israel."[29] With their enemies apparently willing to destroy them at any cost, the Israeli government decided on a bold plan of action.

On June 5 the Israeli Air Force (IAF) launched a surprise morning assault on Egyptian military installations. The strikes on Egypt's airbases quickly crippled their ability to respond: 304 of 419 planes were destroyed. Other IAF missions decimated half of the Syrian military's aircraft, and the modest Jordanian fleet of 28 planes went up in flames.

On the ground the IDF pursued three fronts, sending tanks and thousands of soldiers across borders into Egypt, Syria, and Jordan. Taken completely off guard, defense forces in the three countries were forced to retreat. Meanwhile, Jordanian artillery had been shelling the Mediterranean city of Tel Aviv as well as portions of Jerusalem. But Israeli forces pushed deeply into the West Bank and East Jerusalem, putting an end to the assault. Outgunned and outsmarted, the Jordanian brigades had no choice but to retreat.

The Israeli incursion into Syria had been tentative at first; Syrian soldiers could use the advantage of being perched on the hilly Golan Heights to get the best of the Israeli army. But eyeing complete victory, Israeli forces shelled the Golan and then pushed up the hill. After a day of fierce battle, the Syrians abandoned the hillside. In only six days, the tiny nation of Israel had completely routed its enemies on three sides. The short war left 780 Israelis dead, Jordan suffered 2,000 deaths, Syria lost 700, Egypt buried over 11,000 men, and 4,000 Palestinians died. The Arab world stood shocked by their total defeat. Armies from three countries had been humbled by the upstart Jewish nation. Arab pride, in less than a week, had been felled; utter humiliation took its place.

In stark contrast, Jews around the world celebrated Israel's quick yet decisive defeat of its Arab enemies. The stereotype of the persecuted Jew had, for a time at least, disappeared; pride replaced it. But other Jewish voices suggested that the Six-Day War provided Israel a perfect opportunity to reach out to the Palestinians. Israeli commentator I.F. Stone viewed Israel's victory as a chance to make amends with their Arab counterparts by finding the Palestinians homes and paying them reparations for their earlier losses of property. "Now is a time to right that wrong . . . " he wrote, "and to lay the foundations of a new order in the Middle East in which Israeli and Arab can live in peace."[30]

Few Jews—Israeli or otherwise—lent much credence to Stone's plea. They viewed making any concessions to the Palestinians or Arab countries as a sign of weakness that their enemies would try to exploit. Still, Israel sought long-term security and appeared willing to talk. The United Nations attempted to broker a solution when it drafted and passed Resolution 242. Israel, according to the agreement, would withdraw from the territories they claimed during

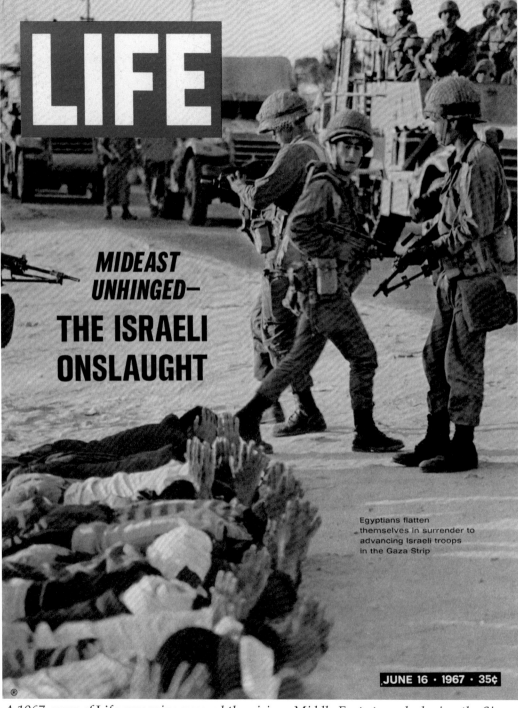

LIFE

MIDEAST UNHINGED—
THE ISRAELI ONSLAUGHT

Egyptians flatten
themselves in surrender to
advancing Israeli troops
in the Gaza Strip

JUNE 16 · 1967 · 35¢

A 1967 cover of Life *magazine exposed the vicious Middle East struggle during the Six-Day War to an international audience.*

Pan-Arabism

I n the early twentieth century a movement called Pan-Arabism began to spread across the Middle East. Pan-Arabism is the belief that Arab people, regardless of the country in which they live, should unite and reject European colonialism. Its proponents began voicing their opinions as early as the 1930s. At the time, Egyptian prime minister Mustafa al-Nahhas tried to unite his people in a widely published manifesto. He criticized Egypt for allowing Great Britain to meddle in its affairs of state: "Egyptians, now is the time to raise your voice against the weakness of Egypt's policy and against the greed and ambition of the British. . . . Let us, one and all, raise our voices to tell all that there are people in Egypt who will not be subjugated." Other cries for Pan-Arabism soon followed, but not until 1952 and the rise of Gamal Abdel Nasser did the Arab world have a leader popular and strong enough to make the vision a reality.

Quoted in Michael Scott Doran, *Pan-Arabism Before Nasser.* New York: Oxford University Press, 2002, p. 20.

the conflict, including the West Bank. The Arab countries would, conversely, recognize Israel's right to exist, something that up to that time all of them had refused to do. Despite the UN's pleas, neither the Arabs nor the Israelis abided by Resolution 242. Israel came to the conclusion that returning the Gaza Strip, West Bank, or any part of Jerusalem would again leave them vulnerable to attack from neighboring Arab nations.

Internal Divisions

Beyond external threats, Israel also had to confront internal divisions among its own populace. Many of the Jewish nation's early Zionist leaders were devout secularists, meaning their religious beliefs were secondary to their greater goals for the nation and Jewish culture as a whole. According to historians William Scott Green and Jed Silverstein, religious leaders at first criticized Zionism's "leaders and . . . the unrealistic impractical nature of the endeavor."[31] They also feared that Zionism would erode traditional Jewish beliefs and religious practices by encouraging Jews to look for redemption, or rescue, in politics rather than religion. On the other hand, many Jews—Conservative and Orthodox, especially—had moved to Israel precisely because they believed that as God's "Chosen People" the land—what they called Eretz Yisrael—

A Jewish man prays outside the Tomb of Abraham at Hebron.

was rightfully theirs. They saw it as their ancient inheritance, as promised in the Hebrew Bible. The West Bank is also considered sacred ground, especially to more religious Jews. But controlling these lands presented complications.

Israel refused to officially annex, or claim, the West Bank and Gaza after the Six-Day War; therefore, neither became part of Israel proper. Consequently, the large Palestinian populations in Gaza and the West Bank remained in legal limbo. Because the territories were not part of a particular country, Israel did not have to grant citizenship to the Palestinians living there. Doing so, the Israeli government believed, would ethnically undermine the Jewish nation.

Yet controlling areas filled mostly with Palestinians and refusing to make them Israeli citizens and allowing them to vote could damage Israel's credibility as a democracy. Israeli leaders were in a quandary, and they knew it. They hoped that for a while at least they could leave these problems unresolved, but they quickly found otherwise.

Religious Zionists wanted Gaza and the West Bank to become permanent parts of the State of Israel, despite Resolution 242. And in April 1968 two of them took the matter into their own hands. Rabbis Eliezer Waldman and Moshe Levinger requested that the Israeli government allow them to celebrate the Passover holiday at Abraham's tomb in the West Bank. They promised to return to Israel after one week. After receiving approval for the visit, the rabbis and their families traveled to Hebron's Park Hotel. But at week's end, Waldman and Levinger refused to leave. Although the UN had deemed permanent Jewish settlements in the West Bank and Gaza illegal, the settlers announced they answered to a higher calling. "God has shown us the way to redeem the Jewish nation,"[32] said Waldman.

Their daring move paid off. Despite international pressure, Israeli officials allowed the settlers to stay for as long as they wanted and vowed to protect them militarily. Other groups soon followed Waldman and Levinger into the Occupied Territories. Thus began the settlement movement, which would continue to grow and, in time, deepen the divide between the Palestinians and Israelis.

Life in the Territories

Soon after Israel captured the Gaza Strip and West Bank in the Six-Day War, Jewish settlers began moving in. For the Palestinians already living there, this often meant immediate eviction by the Israeli military. Many were forced into cramped refugee camps; they had little work and less money to feed their families. Today, daily life in the Territories remains bleak for most Palestinians. Controlled by Israel but not given the rights afforded to those living in Israel proper, Palestinians in the occupied lands have little control over their destinies. Over the years, many young Palestinians living there have, consequently, turned to violence. Hamas and other extremist organizations thrive in places where poverty and hopelessness persist. But even those who have not resorted to terrorism often find their lives at the mercy of forces they cannot control. Fifty-nine-year-old Abu Saqqir was born in the village of al-Hadidiyya. Israeli soldiers frequently search the area for suspected terrorists or use bulldozers to destroy the homes in what they dub military zones. "In my own case, they've demolished my home four times," says Abu Saqqir. "Now, we just have some pieces of wood and a tent to live in."

Quoted in "Israel: Stop Demolishing Palestinian Homes," *Human Rights Watch*, June 12, 2009. www.hrw.org/en/news/2009/06/12/israel-stop-demolishing-palestinian-homes.

Israel after the Six-Day War, 1967.

☐ Before June, 1967

☐ After June, 1967

N
W E
S

LEBANON

SYRIA

Beirut

Damascus

Haifa

Mediterranean Sea

GOLAN HEIGHTS

Tel Aviv

Amman

Jerusalem

Ashkelon

Gaza

DEAD SEA

Port Said

Beersheba

JORDAN

ISRAEL

Suez

Elath

Aqaba

SINAI PENINSULA

Gulf of Suez

SAUDI ARABIA

EGYPT

Sharm-el-Sheikh

Red Sea

War of Attrition and the Death of Nasser

As Israelis debated what to do with the West Bank and Gaza, sporadic clashes between Israel and its Arab neighbors continued. IDF missions along the new borders were frequent; Arab leaders seethed and often sent small bands of fighters to confront Israeli forces.

Egypt's Nasser seemed particularly angry. The Sinai Peninsula and much of the Suez Canal now belonged to Israel, but Nasser continually challenged Israel's control of the areas. In March 1969 he launched a blistering, large-scale offensive against Israeli canal positions. In retaliation, Israel bombarded the Egyptian forces from the air with new and more precise weapons: American-made F-4 Phantoms and A-4 Skyhawks.

The Egyptians, meanwhile, utilized Soviet advisers who provided radar technology and surface-to-air missiles that proved effective in downing Israeli airplanes. The back-and-forth continued well into the spring and summer months with no clear winner. An American-led initiative to broker an end to the conflict failed when Israel refused to retreat to its pre-1967 borders in exchange for proposed peace with Egypt and Jordan. Instead, in early 1970 the Israeli Air Force began bombing Cairo's suburbs, forcing thousands of Egyptians to flee. Negotiations continued, but not until August did Israel finally agree to halt the bombing raids. In return, they retained Gaza and the West Bank.

For Israeli prime minister Golda Meir, further negotiations with a weakened Egypt or the larger Arab world were futile. Going forward, she viewed the best strategy for lasting peace as a "diplomacy of attrition."[33] Since Israel had already proved its military might and captured large swaths of Arab land, she believed that her nation's enemies would realize that Israel was not going to disappear and that, in time, a peace treaty would result.

But in September 1970 the political complexion of Middle East politics changed when Nasser died of a heart attack. His successor, Anwar Sadat, appeared unwilling or politically unable to make official peace with the Jewish state. He spoke to Egyptians of the importance of the moment: "1971 will be the Year of Decision, toward war or peace. This is a problem that cannot be postponed any longer. . . . Everything depends on us. This is neither America's nor the Soviets' war, but our war, deriving from our will and determination."[34]

Despite Sadat's determination, Arab nations were bruised and battered. They had confronted the Israelis hoping to drive them into the Mediterranean Sea and out of the Middle East. They had lost. Although Arab leaders were loath to admit it, the Israelis now commanded one of the world's most powerful militaries. They were not going anywhere.

Chapter Three

Palestinians Find a Voice

The failure of Israel's enemies to drive the Jews out changed the strategic and political landscape of the Middle East. While Arab nations bided their time and waited for another opportunity to challenge the thriving Jewish state, Palestinians began planning their own resistance to Israeli occupation. If the Palestinians were going to have a homeland, they could no longer rely solely on others for help. Instead, they would need a grassroots organization made up of ordinary Palestinians fighting to undermine Israel wherever and whenever possible.

Fatah and the PLO

By the early 1970s the Palestinians who remained in the disputed lands often lived in squalid, cramped refugee camps. Meant to be temporary when first built by the United Nations in the 1940s and 1950s, they had become per-manent housing for hundreds of thousands of the poor.

In addition to the refugee camps in Gaza and the West Bank, thousands of displaced Palestinians had ended up in Jordan; others found residence in Kuwait. As with the Jewish diaspora years before, more Palestinians lived outside of their ancient lands than lived within them. These Palestinians often existed in camps, too, but in these countries a movement began to grow—one that promised to raise the stakes and transform the conflict into an even bloodier war.

Soon after the end of the Six-Day War, small bands of Palestinian guerrillas began roaming the Gaza Strip and Jordan. The best known and armed of these was Fatah, which takes its name from a reverse acronym: Harakat al-Tahrir al-Filistiniya, meaning "conquest" in Arabic. Its emblem is a grenade and crossed rifles over a map of Israel. Founded in 1958, Fatah's early leaders were university graduates living in Kuwait. Meanwhile, in 1964 members of the Arab League, the alliance of Arab countries in the region, helped form the Palestine Liberation Organization (PLO).

While the Arab countries wanted to support the Palestinians in their resistance to Israel, they did not want the Palestinians to work on their own and become too powerful. Thus, the Arab League gave the PLO little real authority at first. Instead, the organization was tightly controlled and managed by the Arab League itself. But after Israel's defeat of Arab forces in the Six-Day War, Palestinians lost faith in the larger Arab world. Arab nations had been of little use in helping the Palestinians claim a homeland, and Palestinian leadership became so frustrated that they broke away from the Arab League.

The PLO claimed its independence and raised its profile when it moved to Jordan in 1967. There, it quickly recruited young men to its cause of a free and independent Palestine. Meanwhile, Fatah, the PLO's largest faction, made a name for itself in March 1968 when its guerrilla fighters battled Israeli troops near the Jordanian village of Karamah. Global news coverage raised the group's profile and led to thousands of young Arabs joining the organization. "If the Palestinians were shamed by the outcome of the 1967 [war]," writes historian Baruch Kimmerling, "they regarded the *Karamah* . . . as a victory over the powerful Israeli armed forces that provided

them with a source of pride and hope."[35] The battle at Karamah was led by a young Palestinian named Yasir Arafat.

Arafat, a Palestinian engineer, had helped found Fatah. In 1969 he was elected chairman of the PLO. The PLO soon became the primary voice of the Palestinian people. In its revised Palestine National Charter, the PLO called for "armed struggle" as the only way of liberating all of Palestine, which meant the lands promised in the old Palestine Mandate. The PLO also rejected Israel's right to exist.

This hard line frustrated Israelis but also made them more determined than

Palestinian Yasir Arafat was elected PLO chairman in 1969.

Oscar and the Palestinians

In 1977 noted British actress and political activist Vanessa Redgrave made the film *Julia*. Based on the life of a woman who was murdered for her antifascist views by the Nazis, Redgrave's performance earned her an Academy Award nomination. Also that year, Redgrave narrated and funded a documentary about the plight of the Palestinians. In the days leading up to the Oscar telecast, the Jewish Defense League (JDL), a hard-line Zionist group led by Rabbi Meir Kahane, spoke out against Redgrave, going so far as to burn effigies of the actress in the streets near where the ceremony was to take place. On Oscar night, Redgrave won the award for best supporting actress. After taking the stage, Redgrave paid tribute to those willing to sacrifice their lives to defeat Nazi Germany forty years before. She also thanked the Academy: "You should be very proud that in the last few weeks you've stood firm and you have refused to be intimidated by the threats of a small bunch of Zionist hoodlums whose behavior is an insult to the stature of Jews all over the world." The shocked audience first booed her speech and then lightly applauded. Later in the broadcast, screenwriter Paddy Chayefsky chided Redgrave for using the Oscars to promote her personal politics. His remarks received thunderous applause.

The Truth Will Set You Free, "Vanessa Redgrave's Oscar Speech," March 21, 2009. http://wakeupfrom yourslumber.blogspot.com/2009/03/vanessa-redgraves-oscar-speech_21.html.

Actresses Vanessa Redgrave (left) and Jane Fonda share a scene in the film Julia.

ever to strengthen their military and prepare for the worst. From their country's founding, Israelis had been forced to deal with neighboring countries that refused to accept their existence. Thousands of people, both Israeli and Arab, had died; Israel was always on its guard against potential threats. Now, an organized internal foe had appeared. For Israelis, the Palestinian phrase "armed struggle" was nothing but code for violence and terrorism through which the Palestinians would try to achieve their goals.

But if the Israelis despised the PLO and all it stood for, average Palestinians rejoiced. Although their political, religious, or social beliefs might differ, this unified vision of a free and independent nation inspired many Palestinians. They swelled with pride when they turned on their televisions and watched Yasir Arafat meet with Arab heads of state that sympathized with the plight of the Palestinians and provided financial assistance to the PLO. In this way, Arafat gave a poor and oppressed people reason to hope that they could confront the Israelis head on.

Black September

Arafat used the media as a major political tool. With his trademark black and white kaffiyeh head scarf and green military uniform, Arafat made a name for himself, in part, by appearing on news programs and in newspapers condemning Israel and demanding a Palestinian state. But Arafat's PLO, working with Fatah and other Palestinian resist-

ance groups, also got attention by planning and committing acts of terrorism.

At the 1972 Summer Olympics in Munich, Germany, for example, a Fatah-affiliated group calling itself Black September hopped a chain-link fence into the Olympic Village. Dressed in gym suits to avoid suspicion, they found the apartments containing sleeping Israeli athletes and entered one using a stolen key. Black September guerrilla Jamal al Gashey relished the opportunity to strike: "I felt very proud that for the first time I was able to confront the Israelis."[36]

The initial confrontation happened quickly. Inside the first apartment, the terrorists were confronted by wrestling coach Moshe Weinberg, whom they shot and seriously wounded. The Palestinians then forced the injured Weinberg to lead them to the other Israelis. Weinberg showed them to apartment three, where the wrestlers and weightlifters slept, hoping the strong men might overpower the terrorists. Upon entering the third apartment, wrestler Yossef Romano—a veteran of the Six-Day War—attacked the guerrillas but was shot. Weinberg and Romano soon bled to death, after which the terrorists threw Weinberg's body out of the apartment's front door and demanded the release of over two hundred Palestinian prisoners from Israeli prisons.

Diplomatically, the Israeli government refused to negotiate for the hostages, fearing that such talks would be interpreted as weakness by their enemies and lead to more acts of terror. Prime

A masked Black September guerrilla stands guard outside an apartment complex at the Olympic Village in Munich. In 1972 eleven Israelis were murdered during the terrorist act.

Minister Golda Meir was also furious at Olympic officials, who initially refused to halt the games: "It is inconceivable," she told the Knesset, or Israeli parliament, "that Olympic competitions should continue while Israeli sportsmen are threatened with murder."[37]

After long hours of waiting for rescue, the remaining nine Israelis were taken at gunpoint by helicopter to the Munich airport; the terrorists had demanded an airplane. Agents from Israel's intelligence agency, Mossad, had flown to Munich prepared to ambush the terrorists and rescue the hostages. In the fire fight at the airport, Mossad shot and killed all but three of the terrorists, but all nine Israelis died when the guerrillas tossed live grenades into the choppers.

The massacre in Munich made headlines around the world. But the personal tragedy for the families of the dead athletes was initially overshadowed by the remorseless terrorists themselves. Germany sent the bodies of the five dead terrorists to Libya, a financial supporter of Black September. There they received a hero's funeral and burial attended by thirty thousand Arabs. The three survivors never stood trial. Instead, they were freed and held a news conference. "We have made our voice heard by the world,"[38] one told the reporters.

Newspapers printed photographs of the masked terrorists, but few people had ever heard of Palestinians before. They did not know what Black September was fighting for and were shocked by the brutal actions at the Olympics. In the summer of 1972, the word "Palestinian" became synonymous with terrorism.

Yom Kippur War and Camp David Accords

Egyptian president Anwar Sadat added his voice to the situation. In choosing between war and peace, he chose war. In public statements, Sadat suggested that war was inevitable and that he stood prepared to sacrifice a million Egyptian lives unless Israel would

An Israeli howitzer pounds enemy positions in Syria during the Yom Kippur War.

abide by Resolution 242 and retreat to its pre-1967 borders.

Despite Sadat's threats, 1972 and much of 1973 passed with no attack. Instead, Sadat pushed diplomacy, calling on a number of European and African states to help pressure Israel and the United States, now one of the Jewish state's key allies. His efforts proved fruitless. Even the Soviet Union refused to intervene in the dispute. Most leaders around the world considered an Egyptian attack on Israel unlikely; Sadat's threats appeared hollow.

Then on October 6, 1973, with the help of Syria, Egypt struck. In the past, the Israelis had appeared well prepared for surprise attacks, but the Egyptians had chosen to strike on Yom Kippur, Judaism's Day of Atonement. Millions sat praying in Israeli synagogues as 80,000 Egyptian soldiers crossed into the Sinai, quickly overwhelming the 436 Israelis defending it.

In the Golan Heights, 1,400 Syrian tanks faced off against 180 Israeli tanks. Completely outnumbered, the Israelis tried to hold off the advancing enemy armies. Israeli commanders called up thousands of reinforcements, and after five days of fierce fighting the Israelis were able to repel the Syrian forces.

Sinai was worse, as the Israeli troops were forced to retreat ten miles from their original position. Yet after days of struggle, Israeli forces regained their footing, with brigades pushing deep into Syria. Meanwhile, Israeli commander Ariel Sharon broke through Egyptian lines in the Sinai and ordered a fierce counterattack. His plan worked, and Israeli soldiers pushed toward Cairo.

Again bested by the Israelis, Egypt and Syria called for a cease-fire, and Israel agreed on October 25; Israeli forces returned to their 1967 borders. But for Israelis, this brief war had come at a higher cost than previous conflicts; 2,688 of their soldiers died in battle, and more than 7,000 were wounded. Israeli citizens wondered why their government had been caught unprepared. As a result of the public outcry, Prime Minister Golda Meir resigned and was replaced by former Israeli military commander Yitzhak Rabin in April 1974.

Political circumstances also changed in Egypt. President Sadat had long sought a stronger relationship with the United States, a key ally of Israel, and now worked to make diplomatic inroads with Rabin's Labor Party. In September 1975 Egypt and Israel agreed to settle their differences peacefully by signing the Sinai Interim Agreement. Then in 1977, after months of negotiations, Sadat took a daring step: He stood before Israel's parliament, the Knesset, and recognized Israel's right to exist—the first Arab power to do so: "We used to reject you," he said, "Yet today I tell you, and I declare to the whole world, that we accept living with you in permanent peace based on justice."[39]

One year after Sadat's historic announcement, he and Israel's new prime minister Menachem Begin agreed to peace at Camp David, the American presidential retreat in Maryland. The terms of the agreement included Israel's return of the Sinai and Egypt's recognition of Israel's borders. U.S. president Jimmy Carter also promised military aid to Egypt. The official treaty was signed in 1979 in Washington, D.C., as Begin and Sadat shook hands.

But peace with Egypt did not coax other Arab nations to fall in line. On the contrary, they dug in their diplomatic heels and convinced the Arab League to rescind Egypt's membership. While Israel learned it could negotiate with, and even trust, an Arab nation once bent on its destruction, Egypt paid a heavy

price for making peace. While reviewing a parade in 1981, Sadat was assassinated. Once again, the bloodshed had only just begun.

PLO's Changing Reputation

While at least one Arab country decided to make peace with Israel, the PLO and Yasir Arafat refused to follow Egypt's lead. A number of Western nations had sympathy for the Palestinian cause, but the Munich massacre and other violent PLO actions alienated many others. In

Security forces in Beirut ready themselves for battle as the Lebanese civil war of 1975 rages on.

the Arab world, too, the PLO's popularity waned. For years, Arab leaders had funded PLO operations, but Arafat spent too much of the money on himself, leading a lavish lifestyle that offended many Muslims. In Jordan, where the PLO had set up operations, the government took steps to curb the organization's power. Armed members of Fatah and other Palestinian groups roamed the streets, armed and willing to challenge the Jordanian government. The PLO members nearly rivaled Jordan's army in terms of sheer manpower. Finally, in desperate fear of being overthrown, the Jordanian officials ordered their troops to confront the PLO. The military action that followed succeeded in crushing PLO militants and forcing them to leave Jordan.

Again without a country from which to launch strikes against Israel, the Palestinian group asked for permission to stay in Egypt or Syria; both countries refused to take them. Lebanon, a country weakened by internal conflict, did not. From Lebanon's southern border with Israel, the PLO was free to carry out attacks and, according to historian Aaron Mannes, "effectively governed portions of the country . . . where they murdered, raped, and tortured Lebanese citizens."[40]

The PLO's presence in Lebanon helped destabilize the already fragile country, which devolved into civil war between Christian and Muslim factions in 1975. Unable to confront Israel's military power directly, Arafat worked to frighten Israelis with cross-border raids which in 1978 resulted in Israel's occupation of parts of southern Lebanon. Although they soon withdrew, the conflict continued to simmer.

War in Lebanon

Most of all, the PLO tried to cause as much friction between the Arab nations and Israel as possible. Signing peace treaties with Israel, such as Egypt had done, did not help the cause of a Palestinian state. "In no way, shape, or form did the PLO want a peace environment to emerge in the Arab-Israeli arena," writes historian David W. Lesch. "It needed the Arab states at war with Israel because that was the only way it had any hope of defeating Israel."[41] By the early 1980s, Lebanon was ground zero for that war, as the PLO continued attacking Israel's northern border.

Then, after agreeing to a cease-fire, the PLO again attacked the Jewish nation. Over the course of eleven months, the PLO killed twenty-nine Israeli civilians and two diplomats. And on June 6, 1982, Israel retaliated by launching a massive military operation into southern Lebanon. The PLO was no match for the well-armed Israelis. But Israel was not fighting a war against the country of Lebanon, according to Israeli defense minister and former general Ariel Sharon; it was, instead, creating a twenty-five-mile (40km) buffer zone, or distance, between Lebanon and Israel so that the PLO could no longer attack.

Journalist Thomas Friedman covered the war in Lebanon and believed

Sharon had other plans for the IDF: "Sharon did not play games with his enemies," Friedman writes. "He killed them."[42] By the middle of June, Sharon's ruthless determination won Israel more than a buffer zone. With tanks and soldiers surrounding Beirut, Lebanon's capital city, Sharon seemed intent on destroying the PLO once and for all.

Outgunned and outmanned, the PLO nonetheless continued fighting, but they were losing the battle. In August the PLO moved nearly fourteen thousand troops from the area; Arafat, meanwhile, boarded a ship bound for Tunisia in Northern Africa. Arafat had escaped with his life, if just barely. With his reputation in the Arab world shattered, he tried to regroup, but the PLO's influence continued to wane. In its place rose more radical factions of Muslim resisters. Chief among them was Hezbollah, a Lebanese political and paramilitary organization, which would soon introduce a terrifying new tactic and export it for the war against Israel.

Worsening Situation

Outside attacks against Israel ceased for the moment, but the situation inside

Supplies are ferried to a southern Lebanon army encampment by an Israeli helicopter in 1982.

Life in the Settlements

When Yael Simckes's four children take the bus to school they do so behind bulletproof glass. As residents in a Gush Etzion settlement called Elazar in the West Bank, the family lives under daily threat. But Simckes and her family have lived in Elazar for over a decade and have no plans to move, even after a 2005 attack nearby killed three Israelis. In fact, twice as many families reside in the settlement now than when Simckes and her husband Daniel moved in. The housing is affordable and the short drive to Jerusalem or Tel Aviv makes commuting to work easy and convenient. Residents clearly prefer it to the hustle-bustle of large Israeli cities. The self-contained religious community includes a school and synagogue, and Simckes says that the people of the Yishuv are like extended family: They rely on one another to survive and thrive in spite of the threats from Palestinians as well as their own government. Still, Simckes fears the day her children grow up and have to go to war for a land they believe rightfully belongs to them. "You have to have a tremendous amount of faith to live here," she says, "but I wouldn't live anywhere else."

Quoted in Sarah Sirota, "Exclusive Report: Life on a West Bank Settlement," *Jewish Post*, 2008. www.jewishpost.com/news/Life-on-a-West-Bank-Settlement.html.

had become more complicated than ever. After Rabbis Levinger and Waldman founded the Kiryat Arba settlement in 1968, dozens of other settlements sprouted throughout the West Bank and Gaza Strip. In many cases Israel's Labor and Likud parties had won political favor among voters by encouraging new Israeli settlers with financial incentives and a promise of protection by soldiers. And when necessary, leaders ordered the expulsion of Palestinians from their land.

Chief supporter of the settlement movement was Ariel Sharon. By 1987 his efforts had resulted in a dramatic shift. Thirty percent of Gaza and 50 percent of the West Bank now belonged to Israel. But no longer were all settlements lonely outposts, far from Israel's largest cities; now, many of them served as virtual suburbs of Israel's larger cities such as Tel Aviv and Jerusalem.

While Israeli living space had grown, the Palestinians found themselves living on less and less land. The two sides tolerated one another, if only barely. The Palestinians had little choice. Controlled by Israel and unable to trade with other Arab nations, the Palestinians turned to the Israelis for work. The

Israelis, conversely, relied on cheap Palestinian labor to serve them at restaurants, clean their houses, and build their settlements.

The Palestinians resented the low wages and the work itself. The money they earned enabled them to feed their families, but building settlements on land they believed the Israelis stole from them made them feel humiliated and worthless. Each night they returned to ramshackle, forty-year-old refugee camps, while the Israelis prospered.

Based on past experience, Israelis had a difficult time trusting the Palestinians. For protection they set up military checkpoints where each day nearly 200,000 Palestinians passed into Israeli-controlled areas to go to work. Few incidents of resistance occurred. The PLO remained mostly in exile; its remnants planned attacks on Israelis from time to time, but Israeli security forces kept a tight rein on the movements of average Palestinians. Shin Bet, Israel's domestic security agency (like the FBI), often hired them as informers to tell them about ongoing plots or detained those they deemed suspicious.

These tactics made the Palestinians feel even more like prisoners in a land that they believed was supposed to belong to them. Bilal, a Palestinian boy, lived in the Jabalia camp. He makes no attempt to hide the bitterness he felt toward the Israelis: "All of the suffering we had was because of the occupation," he says. "The Israeli army despised the whole population."[43]

Intifada

Bilal's view was common among Palestinians. With few rights or opportunities to prosper, an entire population seethed. And on December 8, 1987, it exploded. That day, an Israeli truck driver took a wrong turn into a Gaza neighborhood and ran over four Palestinian workers. While the deaths were most likely the result of an accident, some Palestinians believed otherwise. On December 6, just two days before, an Israeli store owner had been stabbed to death. Rumors swirled that the trucking accident was an act of revenge. On December 9 a group of teens hurled rocks at Israeli soldiers, who retaliated by shooting seventeen-year-old Hatem Abu Sisi.

According to their usual practice, Israeli soldiers planned to take Sisi's body and bury it at night to avoid Palestinian protest. But when the troops arrived at the refugee camp to take Sisi's body, they were again showered with stones. Riots ensued and quickly spread to other camps. So began what came to be known as the intifada, which literally means "to shake off slumber."

Mohammed began throwing rocks at Israeli soldiers when he was only a young boy, but he regrets none of his actions: "When you're ten years old and saw what the Jews did and how they shot at us, we couldn't be numb. . . . We were shot at many times, but that only made us attack more. Yes, I was shot twice. We couldn't stand still seeing our brothers and neighbors bleeding. We have to liberate Palestine and its people."[44]

The rock throwing and outright hostility frightened many Israelis. For the first time, the Palestinians had developed an identity and sense of nationalism. The Israelis, meanwhile, were at a loss. How could they combat Palestinian forces comprised mostly of young boys? If they ignored the harassment they might seem vulnerable and weak; if they responded with gunfire the world would criticize them for hurting children. For the most part, they responded with rubber bullets and arrests of suspected attackers.

But other, even more serious questions arose: Were the Israelis willing to give Palestinians the Territories in exchange for peace? And if they did, could their safety and security be guaranteed? No easy answers existed, for them or for Palestinian leadership.

Arafat watched the intifada unfold. The PLO renounced terrorism and recognized Israel's right to exist in 1988,

Palestinian demonstrators throw rocks at Israeli soldiers during the intifada that began in late 1987.

but a series of world events convinced Arafat that something had to change in the relationship between Israel and the Palestinians.

Global Changes

When the Cold War ended in 1989, the Soviet Union dissolved. The Communist superpower had been a longtime supporter of Arab nations and of the Palestinians in particular. Without this force supporting them, Arafat felt his power weakened.

For Arafat, another cause for alarm was the founding of a rival Palestinian group, Hamas, which means "fighting force" in Arabic. Made up mostly of men who had grown up in the Occupied Territories, Hamas took an even harder line against Israel than the PLO. They also made inroads with ordinary Palestinians by setting up medical centers and schools.

During the intifada, Hamas began winning the hearts and minds of the Palestinian people, serving its poorest citizens but demanding loyalty in return. In years to come, Hamas's strategy would win them respect among Palestinians while changing the lives of ordinary Israelis.

The PLO had already changed the lives of Palestinians. By lobbying Arab and European nations for support and daring to confront the powerful nation of Israel, the PLO forced the world to recognize the cause of Palestinian statehood. While PLO methods were often criticized, few could deny the transformation: A people once thought helpless and politically destitute now had a voice, and others were listening.

Chapter Four

A Chance for Peace and a Return to Violence

The early 1990s provided both sides in the Israeli-Palestinian conflict a unique opportunity: The political atmosphere in Israel suggested that ordinary Israelis were looking for their leaders to take bolder action to stem the tide of Palestinian violence and work toward ending years of bloodshed. Palestinian leadership, meanwhile, also recognized the need to solve the crisis or risk losing the support of its people to more violent factions willing to kill as many innocent Israelis as possible. Fear also played a vital role in bringing both sides to the bargaining table. The world was about to change, and neither side knew exactly who to trust anymore.

Oslo Peace Process

The 1990 Gulf War made both sides of the Israeli-Palestinian conflict nervous. The Palestinians supported Iraqi dictator Saddam Hussein in the war, while many of their Arab brethren sided with the United States in removing Hussein's invading forces from Kuwait. This development also worried Israel, which feared the United States would build even closer ties to Israel's enemies. With so much political uncertainty in the region, both sides in the Israeli-Palestinian conflict looked for a solution to their own long-standing problems.

A first attempt at lasting peace occurred in 1991 during the Madrid Peace Conference in Spain. After a time, the negotiations moved to Washington, D.C., but the back-and-forth produced little of lasting value. Still, Israelis and Palestinians realized that they had to keep trying to find a peaceful way forward. The Palestinians believed they had the best chance yet to win a Palestinian state; the Israelis did not want to return to the violence of the intifada. "The most significant consequence of the Intifada," wrote scholar Robert Owen Freedman, "is that it convinced almost everyone that the status quo was no longer a viable solution."[45] Rabin took particular notice. Born in Jerusalem in 1922, Rabin first trained as an irrigation engineer, but after taking courses in military strategy he changed his major, and that changed his life.

Rabin first saw action in Lebanon as a member of Haganah. Later, he led forces during the first Arab-Israeli War in 1948. As with many other Israeli military men, he eventually made the leap into politics, serving as minister of defense and, in 1974, prime minister after Meir's resignation.

Upon his election to a second term as prime minister in 1992, he canceled plans for six thousand Israeli housing units in the West Bank—a bold step. He also made a negotiated peace with the

Leaders (from left to right) Yitzhak Rabin, Bill Clinton, and Yasir Arafat pose at the White House on September 13, 1993, immediately following the Oslo Accords agreement.

Palestinians a priority of his Labor Party. Historian William B. Quandt described Rabin as "a man who just might be regarded by Israelis as combining the right dose of realism and toughness to see them through the next phase of the negotiating process."[46] Thus, with the PLO more open to negotiations than ever before, Israel agreed to secret negotiations in Oslo, Norway, in 1992. The clandestine meetings were meant to avoid the glare of news media. Direct talks—Israeli to Palestinian—were believed to be the only way of getting a deal done.

The accord being hammered out would provide the Palestinians a chance to gradually run their own government, to be called the Palestinian Authority, and serve their own people in the Occupied Territories. In return, the Palestinians would fully recognize the state of Israel and guarantee protection from terrorist attacks. In the longer term, talks would continue to work out which parts of the Territories and Jerusalem the Palestinians would control and whether Palestinian refugees could someday return home.

On September 13, 1993, Rabin and Arafat shook hands to seal the Oslo Accords. The ceremony took place on the South Lawn of the White House in Washington, D.C., with American president Bill Clinton and three thousand invited guests looking on. Although it had played a limited role in the final agreement between the Israelis and Palestinians, the United States hosted the event because of its past support for Middle East peace. Many onlookers rejoiced, while others wondered how long it could last. Scholar and activist Edward Said, for one, believed that Oslo would only weaken the PLO and its ability to win a Palestinian state. Rather than working in resistance to Israeli occupation, Said saw the PLO working with Israel to continue it. "The PLO will become Israel's enforcer," he said, "an instrument of the Occupation."[47]

Massacre at the Mosque

Baruch Goldstein was violently opposed to the PLO and what it stood for, and he believed himself an instrument of God. Born into an Orthodox Jewish family in Brooklyn, New York, Goldstein earned a medical degree before emigrating to Israel and serving in the IDF. A long-time member of the Jewish Defense League, Goldstein held extremely conservative views, and the agreement to hand over control of Gaza and Jericho to the Palestinians drove him over the edge.

On February 25, 1994, Goldstein donned military fatigues and made his way to the Cave of the Patriarchs, a shrine considered holy by both Jews and Muslims but controlled by the Israeli military. He had chosen Purim, the Jewish holiday that commemorates deliverance of the Jews from their enemies. Muslims, meanwhile, were observing Ramadan, a month-long period during which the faithful ask for God's forgiveness of their sins. During the day, believers refrain from eating and drinking and spend more of their

Prayer carpets at the Ibrahim Mosque are covered in blood following the massacre of twenty-nine worshippers by Baruch Goldstein.

time praying. Upon arriving at the Cave of the Patriarchs, Goldstein entered a part of the chamber used by Muslims as a mosque. Moaz, a Palestinian Muslim, was twelve at the time and remembers what happened next: "We were kneeling in prayer when the Jewish settler came into the mosque. The first grenade he threw exploded next to the Imam [religious leader]. The second grenade exploded in the middle of the people praying. And then the settler, who was dressed as a soldier, started shooting."[48]

The mosque erupted in chaos, as screaming worshippers ran in all directions trying to escape Goldstein's assault. The walls of the shrine were spattered in blood; bodies fell to the ground in piles. Finally, a handful of men ran at Goldstein and beat him to death with a fire extinguisher. Twenty-nine Palestinians died; dozens were injured.

Soon after, Israel's Knesset banned Jewish groups they deemed capable of terrorism. While most Israelis were shocked and outraged by the attack in Hebron, extreme factions within the country celebrated the massacre and hailed Goldstein as a hero. His tomb at Kiryat Arba reads, "Here lies the saint,

Suicide Bombing

Suicide bombing is hardly a new phenomenon. When eleventh-century assassins murdered their rivals, their actions brought almost immediate execution. During the Vietnam War in the 1960s and early 1970s, Vietcong guerrillas would commonly carry bombs into American military areas and blow themselves up, taking American soldiers with them. In 1981 Hezbollah militants in Lebanon attacked the Iraq embassy; two years later, suicide bombers drove a truck packed with explosives into the U.S. Embassy in Beirut, killing 241 Marines and 58 French paratroopers. This action convinced the United States to leave Lebanon and convinced the perpetrators that suicide bombing worked. Terrorist organizations around the world soon borrowed the tactic, including al Qaeda, which on September 11, 2001, sent nineteen men on an unprecedented suicide mission: Hijack four airplanes and fly them into the World Trade Center, the Pentagon, and the Capitol in Washington, D.C. The resulting attacks killed three thousand people. Inexpensive, easy to plan, and terrifying to victims, the lure for extremists with a political agenda is clear. But why would a young man or woman agree to be a suicide bomber? According to researcher Yoram Schweitzer, motivations include "personal psychological hardships; despair and uncontrollable eagerness for revenge; and specific goals of personal glory."

Yoram Schweitzer, "Suicide Bombers," *Wide Angle*, PBS, June 18, 2004. www.pbs.org/wnet/wideangle/shows/suicide/index.html.

Rescue workers swarm to the ruins of the U.S. embassy in Beirut following the 1983 suicide bombing attack.

Dr. Baruch Kappel Goldstein, blessed be the memory of the righteous and holy man, may the Lord avenge his blood, who devoted his soul to the Jews, Jewish religion and Jewish land. His hands are innocent and his heart is pure. He was killed as a martyr of God."[49]

A book, published later, further praises Goldstein. Titled *Baruch Hagever [Baruch, the Man]: A Memorial Volume for Dr. Baruch Goldstein, the Saint, May God Avenge His Blood*, the book's various essays take pains to justify in writing Goldstein's murderous behavior. The lead essay, written by extremist rabbi Yitzhak Ginzburg, urges readers to consider not only the negative but what he considers the positive aspects of Goldstein's rampage. Ginzburg stresses Goldstein's deep religious convictions and his desire to save the lives of Jews. Ginzburg also predicts a coming Arab pogrom, or hate crime, against Israelis that Goldstein's act had helped prevent or minimize. In this light, he argues, the massacre was honorable. "It simply seems," he writes, "that the life of Israel is worth more than the life of the Gentile [non-Jew]."[50] Ginzburg's views are not unique among Conservative Jews, yet they promise to create an even bigger divide between Israelis who want the West Bank and Gaza at any cost and those willing to trade those lands for peace.

Control

Despite the tragedy at the Cave of the Patriarchs, the agreement made in Oslo continued as planned. In May 1994 Israeli troops officially handed over much of the Gaza Strip and Jericho to the new Palestinian Authority. Fourteen months later, the Palestinian Authority held control of roughly 3 percent of the Territories. But while the Palestinians controlled a great majority of the population, they still held little land. The economic incentives Israel provided, including a transfer of Palestinian tax money to the Authority and the building of a new port near Gaza, could not completely diminish long-standing hostility toward the Jewish state.

When Arafat returned from exile in the summer of 1994, Palestinians greeted him as a hero and their new president. Less than two years later, Palestinians went to the polls and elected representatives to fill their Palestinian Legislative Council, or Parliament. Fatah members filled most of the initial seats. Never before had average Palestinians controlled their destinies. The Authority, along with Israel's help, had begun to create an imperfect but functioning democracy with courts of law and the PLO flag to wave.

Still, the apparent progress between the two sides could not mask the fissures in the peace. Some Palestinians wanted complete access to and ownership of the Territories and seemed unwilling to allow Israelis to have any of it. Others living outside the Territories wanted the "right of return" question for Palestinian refugees settled immediately.

Groups like Hamas also refused to disavow terrorism as a means to achieve their goal of destroying Israel at any cost. They and other Palestinian groups, including Islamic Jihad, began

Policemen and shop owners search through rubble after a suicide bombing attack on a Jewish market.

a campaign of suicide bombings that lasted for two years and killed one hundred people. Suicide bombers typically strap explosives, sometimes packed with nails, to themselves. They then walk into a crowded market or restaurant and detonate the explosives, killing themselves and scores of others in the process. The concept was not new. The Japanese had used a similar tactic at the end of World War II when kamikaze fighter pilots smashed their planes into American battleships, desperately trying to cause as much damage and loss of life as possible.

The random nature of the bombings frightened Israelis and resigned them to renewed warfare. "I'm not angry," says one Israeli mother whose son was seriously injured in a suicide attack: "It's a war. I know it's a war. I hope it's going to be peace in Israel and at last we'll be in peace, real peace. It's a terrible cost. I know that they [Palestinians] fill their minds in hate. And I know they're growing up hating. . . . How can you be angry? They are not normal people."[51]

While most Israelis initially supported the Oslo Accords, suicide bombings shook their faith in the agreement. They distrusted and detested Arafat for his past PLO activity and feared that once Palestinians had their own country they would grow stronger and one day attack Israel and try taking all of the land.

A Chance for Peace and a Return to Violence ■ 59

Other Israelis, especially those living in conservative settlements like Kiryat Arba, refused to compromise. They claimed that the nation should annex the Territories, keeping them under the complete control of Israel. These and like-minded Orthodox Jews despised the Oslo Accords and believed that Rabin and his Labor Party had disobeyed God and would, in time, abandon the idea of settlements, and them, altogether. Like Baruch Goldstein, they were willing to go to extreme measures, if necessary.

Rabbi Shlomo Goren, Israel's former chief rabbi, rejected the idea of settlement removal out of hand. Any attempt to evict settlers in Hebron, he suggests, is a criminal act. "We have to give our life in the struggle against this vicious plan of the government of Israel," he says, "which relies on the Arabs for its majority, and be ready to die rather than allow the destruction of Hebron."[52] Other West Bank settlers echoed Goren's hard line against the Israeli government and spoke of making the ultimate sacrifice to protect land they believed was theirs.

Assassination

Twenty-five-year-old Yigal Amir was indeed willing to die for Hebron and other parts of the West Bank, but he first had a job to do. On the evening of Saturday, November 4, 1995, the young Israeli said his nightly prayers and then showered and shaved. Before leaving home, Amir loaded his Beretta 84F semiautomatic pistol, stuffed it into his pants, and looked at his watch. He had plenty of time.

Amir then caught the bus to Kings of Israel Square in Tel Aviv. When he arrived at about 9:00 P.M., the peace rally was well under way. Thousands crowded the square, waving the flag of Israel and chanting slogans about nonviolence. By 9:10 P.M. Amir had reached the VIP parking lot. He went largely unnoticed and stood by the square's main stairway. At about 9:50, Prime Minister Yitzhak Rabin finished giving a speech to the crowd and descended the stairs on his way to his heavily armored car. Amir stepped in front of Rabin and fired, hitting the prime minister in the chest at point-blank range. Bodyguards rushed Rabin to the hospital, but the seventy-three-year-old leader died an hour and twenty minutes later.

For decades, the most serious threats to Israeli security had come from Arabs. But now, the extreme right wing of Israeli society threatened to destroy the peace process and divide Israel as never before. After his arrest, Yigal Amir justified his assassination of Rabin on religious grounds, believing the prime minister was too willing to give away land that God had promised to Jews. "I have been studying the Talmud [part of the Hebrew bible] all my life," he told police. "I have all the data."[53]

Writer Steven Bayme strongly disagrees with the assassin's logic that religion drove him to murder Yitzhak Rabin. "Effective Jewish education requires a constant balance between particular Jewish needs and universal imperatives,"

Israelis hold a large portrait of assassinated prime minister Yitzhak Rabin. Rabin was slain by Israeli right-wing extremist Yigal Amir in 1995.

says Bayme. "The mantle of Torah cannot be permitted to justify hatred."[54]

In the days and months after the assassination, people around the world, Jew and non-Jew, added their voices to the dialogue about the future of Israel. The American Jewish Committee urged that Jews recognize and acknowledge their differences but return to what ultimately unites them: history, culture, faith.

Collapse

Calls for unity were not completely ignored. Three years after Oslo, Israelis could agree on one thing: Palestinian terrorism must stop. Many had been willing to give Palestinians their own independent nation, but now, with Israelis dying, attitudes were changing. The anger over suicide bombings also affected Israeli politics. Rabin's successor, Shimon Peres, bore the brunt of Israeli rage because he helped negotiate the Oslo Accords.

The political climate provided a perfect opportunity for a politician willing to talk tough with the Palestinians, and in 1996, Benjamin Netanyahu did just that. The Likud Party candidate demanded an end to the terrorism. The peace process would not proceed, he said, until the safety of Israeli citizens could be guaranteed. This approach worked, and in May he narrowly defeated Peres to become prime minister.

For most Palestinians, Netanyahu's win was their loss. Even before Netanyahu took office, settlers had flocked to the West Bank and Gaza from Israel proper. At the time of the Madrid Peace Conference in 1991, the settlers numbered roughly 75,000; in 1996 their number had increased to 147,000. Netanyahu did nothing to curb this frantic growth. Instead, his Likud government funded dozens of construction projects linking settlements with one another by road and creating barriers that made daily life more difficult for Palestinians living in the Territories. The new prime minister also refused to relinquish any more land to the Palestinian Authority, as the Oslo Accords promised.

Then on September 24, 1996, the Israeli government, with Netanyahu's okay, permitted archaeologists to open a tunnel

Benjamin Netanyahu speaks to a congregation in New York, just months prior to being elected prime minister of Israel.

under the Temple Mount, a place sacred to Jews and Muslims. The Temple Mount is the site of two ancient Jewish temples. The ruins of the second temple still stand and are known as the Western Wall, or Wailing Wall. Muslims refer to the Temple Mount as the Noble Sanctuary, the place where their prophet, Muhammad, ascended to heaven.

After Israel announced plans to excavate the nearby tunnel, the Palestinian Authority spread rumors that the dig was really part of a plan to destroy the al-Aqsa Mosque that sits within the Noble Sanctuary. As a result, riots broke out in Gaza, the West Bank, and Jerusalem, with Israeli riot police fighting with Palestinians outraged by the act. This Tunnel War killed 85 Palestinians and 16 Israelis; 1,200 Palestinians were hurt, as were 87 Israelis.

Palestinians vented their frustration not only because the tunnel was being dug but also because they believed that

Israel had somehow cheated them in the peace process. While the Palestinians offered Israel recognition and a halt to terrorism, the Israelis had promised only to one day negotiate what the Palestinians desired: return of refugees, control of all the Occupied Territories, and partial control of Jerusalem. With their demands now apparently pushed aside, many Palestinians supported the use of terrorism to achieve their goals. To them, the PLO seemed impotent and corrupt: Arafat's government squandered or stole at least $400 million yearly, and little political progress was being made.

Meanwhile, Arafat's chief rival, Hamas, expanded its operations. Now a decade old, it continued building schools and hospitals, providing a lifeline to thousands of poor Palestinians in the Territories and building a base of loyal followers willing to die as martyrs in suicide missions against Israel. At the Alshariyeh Boys School in Hebron, the children spoke out about the damaged peace process and pledged their support for Hamas. When asked, none were surprised that at least

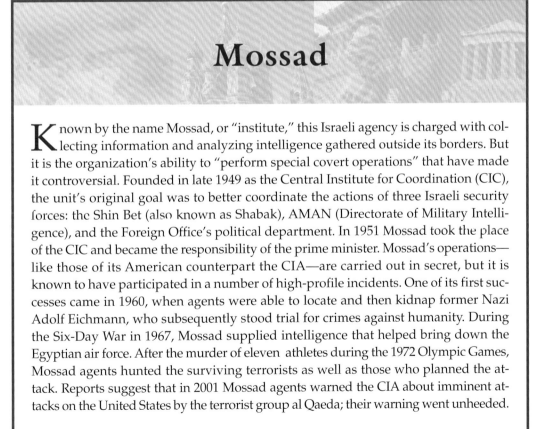

Mossad

Known by the name Mossad, or "institute," this Israeli agency is charged with collecting information and analyzing intelligence gathered outside its borders. But it is the organization's ability to "perform special covert operations" that have made it controversial. Founded in late 1949 as the Central Institute for Coordination (CIC), the unit's original goal was to better coordinate the actions of three Israeli security forces: the Shin Bet (also known as Shabak), AMAN (Directorate of Military Intelligence), and the Foreign Office's political department. In 1951 Mossad took the place of the CIC and became the responsibility of the prime minister. Mossad's operations—like those of its American counterpart the CIA—are carried out in secret, but it is known to have participated in a number of high-profile incidents. One of its first successes came in 1960, when agents were able to locate and then kidnap former Nazi Adolf Eichmann, who subsequently stood trial for crimes against humanity. During the Six-Day War in 1967, Mossad supplied intelligence that helped bring down the Egyptian air force. After the murder of eleven athletes during the 1972 Olympic Games, Mossad agents hunted the surviving terrorists as well as those who planned the attack. Reports suggest that in 2001 Mossad agents warned the CIA about imminent attacks on the United States by the terrorist group al Qaeda; their warning went unheeded.

Mossad, "About Us," 2009. www.mossad.gov.il/Eng/AboutUs.aspx.

two suicide bombers came from Hebron. "If the attacks continue," one student said, "then finally they may bring results to evicting the Jews from our land. And it will become our land."[55]

Yet the continued attacks only prompted a stronger response from the Israeli government. Military forces destroyed the homes of suspected terrorists, killing innocent neighbors in the process. Netanyahu also imposed strict curfews and clamped down on checkpoints through which Palestinians passed to enter Israel.

Attacks led to harsh retaliation, which led to more attacks until October 1998, when Netanyahu and Sharon, his foreign minister, joined Arafat at the Wye River Plantation in Maryland. Working with American president Bill Clinton, the men eventually agreed to continue the Oslo plan and relinquish another 13 percent of the West Bank to the Palestinian Authority. Upon returning home, Sharon told Israel Radio listeners to take what land they could before it was too late: "Grab more hills, expand the territory. Everything that's grabbed, will be in our hands. Everything we don't grab will be in their hands."[56]

Camp David

The agreement signed in Maryland alienated conservative supporters of Netanyahu and Sharon. Despite Sharon's radio interview, they felt that any compromise only weakened Israel's position. This outcry against the prime minister's government led to a new election in 1999, in which Netanyahu was defeated. Labor's Ehud

Barak, the new prime minister, initially disappointed Palestinians, who hoped the leader might work for a breakthrough in the conflict. In his victory speech, he offered no olive branch of peace, saying, "We will not give up Jerusalem; we will not give up the Jordan Valley; we will not allow refugees to return; and we will not go back to the borders of 1967."[57]

In July 2000, though, Barak pushed for a new and final accord with the Palestinians. Clinton eagerly agreed to host a meeting between Barak and Arafat at Camp David, where, two decades before, Israel and Egypt had agreed to peace. Arafat joined the talks more reluctantly and only attended under pressure from Clinton. The United States was too pro-Israel, he believed, and would not be an honest broker. He did not trust the Israelis either and felt they would never give up control of the entire Occupied Territories. Before the talks officially began, Arafat made but one demand: If negotiations failed, he would not be blamed.

The three men and their advisers met from July 11–24 to work out an agreement. Barak's team offered their counterparts 91 percent of the West Bank and the entire Gaza Strip, control over East Jerusalem as the capital of a Palestinian state, and financial reparations to refugees for their confiscated property. In return, Israel demanded that Arafat and the Palestinians demilitarize, or lay down their weapons. The Israelis also asked for the right to control Palestinian airspace in order to discourage

Palestinian missile attacks and the right to deploy the Israeli military into the Palestinian state if threatened. Finally, Israel requested that an international force be stationed in the Jordan Valley to keep the peace.

Arafat rejected the proposal. "Arafat was simply incapable of making a decision on such fateful matters," wrote scholar Amnon Lipkin-Shahak. "This inability was clearly reflected in his public statements to the effect that making such a decision was tantamount to giving up his life, that if he made such concessions, he was as good as dead."[58]

Second Intifada

The breakdown of the Camp David summit did prove fatal for any last vestiges of the Oslo Accords. What seemed so close now appeared farther away than ever before. The endless cycle of raised hopes and dashed dreams embittered Israelis and Palestinians who doubted peace was even possible.

Likud Party leader Sharon did not make his reputation as a peacemaker. And on September 28, 2000, he enraged Palestinians with his visit to the al Haram al Sharif, or Noble Sanctuary. Located at the top of the Temple Mount, the Noble Sanctuary was partially controlled by the Palestinians. But, protected by one thousand heavily armed police officers, Sharon strode into the sanctuary, calling his visit a gesture of peace. Most Palestinians instead viewed his gesture as a proverbial slap in the face. They believed Sharon was flaunting Israel's power and control over Jerusalem, which included their holy site.

The following day, Palestinians stood on top of the mount and hurled stones at Jews praying at the Western Wall, also known as the Wailing Wall, down below. Israeli troops responded with gunfire that killed seven. Soon after, riots erupted and the second intifada had begun. Known to Palestinians as the al Aqsa intifada, after the mosque within the Noble Sanctuary, it proved far more violent than the first.

Two day after Sharon's bold action, Israeli soldiers and Palestinian demonstrators began firing at one another in Jerusalem. Twelve-year-old Palestinian boy Muhammad al-Durrah was caught in the cross fire. Despite the efforts of his father who rushed to his aid and tried to save him, the terrified child was riddled with bullets and killed. TV cameras captured the harrowing scene, and Arab television stations played the footage almost continuously. Exactly whose bullets killed Muhammad al-Durrah remains unclear. Rumors that the whole incident was staged by Palestinians arose. But regardless of the questions surrounding the incident, al-Durrah's violent death only fueled Palestinian anger against their Israeli occupiers.

A few weeks later, Israeli outrage peaked as well when two Israeli soldiers were detained in the Palestinian town of Ramallah. A vicious mob soon broke into police headquarters where the soldiers were being held, killed them, and mutilated their bodies. The

Israeli right-wing opposition leader Ariel Sharon (middle) is flanked by security guards during his controversial visit to the Haram al-Sharif, at the top of the Temple Mount.

violence had quickly gone from bad to worse, and neither side knew exactly how to stop it.

At the beginning of the decade, Palestinians and Israelis had reasons to be hopeful. During the Oslo Accords, the two sides came closer than ever to forging peace and finding a way to tolerate one another. But by the decade's end, extremism trumped moderation, and the Middle East again slipped into chaos and violence.

Chapter Five

The Road Forward

Rarely had the relationship between Palestinians and Israelis been as contentious as at the beginning of the new millennium. The age of Arafat was waning, as more violent Palestinian groups rose in opposition to Israel. For its part, Israel seemed prepared to take the bold step of withdrawing from parts of the Occupied Territories.

Yet withdrawal would come at a political price and further alienate religious Israelis who believe God had given the West Bank to them. First and foremost, Israel had to find a way to combat young Palestinians willing to sacrifice their lives to destroy the Jewish state and its people.

The Uprising Continues

As the second intifada exploded onto the streets of Israel, Gaza, and the West Bank, Ehud Barak did not know what to do. With hundreds already dead and no end in sight, the uprising continued into early 2001. Initially, Barak tried closing borders between Israel and the Occupied Territories, but Palestinian attackers still got through. He also attempted to stem the violence by cutting off Israeli funding to the Palestinian Authority. But neither of these tactics worked; the violence continued.

In the minds of Israelis, Barak had failed during the Camp David Summit, and now he was failing to put a stop to the atrocious violence of the second intifada. In February, Israelis went to the polls and elected Sharon as their new leader. According to journalist Tony Karon, the former general was extremely unpopular in Israel. But his election was a sign of "Israel's deep disillusionment with the peace process. Sharon didn't win," wrote Karon, "as much as Barak lost."[59]

Upon his election, Sharon pledged a hard line against Israel's enemies. He

Palestinians search for their belongings within their ravaged homes in the southern Gaza Strip after Israeli forces razed the refugee camp.

reversed Barak's policies: Israel would not give over control of any part of Jerusalem; settlements in the Territories would not shrink, they would expand. Most important, no peace could occur until all terrorism ceased. The former general despised Arafat and devised a new strategy to halt the violence and perhaps Arafat himself: Each time a terrorist detonated a bomb, the IDF would destroy a PA building.

By putting extreme pressure on the Palestinian government, Sharon believed violence against Israelis would stop. Sharon did not stop there. He ordered the use of new tactics such as bombs and targeted killing of militant leaders. He also sought the terrorists themselves and was willing to demolish whole Palestinian neighborhoods to find them.

While militarily effective, these methods brought fresh concerns from many Israelis. Innocent Palestinians were often killed or seriously injured during such attacks. Commentators and citizens wondered whether commanders were going too far. Editors at *Ha'aretz*, a leading Israeli newspaper, wrote, "the IDF . . . is turning into a killing machine whose efficiency is awe-inspiring, yet shocking."[60] Newspapers were not the only voices of dissent. In an official condemnation of Israeli military actions, four former Shin Bet members expressed their deep

Palestinian Christians

Not all Palestinians are Muslim. Roughly 50,000 Palestinian Christians live in Gaza and the West Bank; 175,000 of them live in Israel. Like so many Jews and Muslims, these Christian families have refused to leave a land that contains many of their holiest sites. The Temple Mount in Jerusalem is where, according to their faith, Jesus spoke out against the Hebrew priests who ran the Temple and raged against the money changers and their "den of thieves." The Church of the Nativity in Bethlehem is built over the cave in which they believe their savior was born. This rich history, though, cannot hide the fact that Palestinian Christians in the Holy Land often feel forgotten or squeezed out of a conflict fought primarily between Jews and Muslims. In the last few decades more have decided to leave for places like Canada, Australia, or the United States. Those who do

Hordes of Palestinian Christians observe Good Friday in Jerusalem.

stay are often older people with neither the money nor the energy to move. Yet as this population dies out, few may be willing to take their place. "In one Jerusalem parish," writes journalist Charles M. Sennott, "there were not enough young Christian men left to carry a casket at a funeral."

Charles M. Sennott, *The Body and the Blood*. New York: Public Affairs, 2001, p. xi.

concern over the execution of Israel's response to the intifada. "We are behaving disgracefully,"[61] they wrote.

Arafat, on the other hand, was caught between Israel's dominant military and his chief competitors, Hamas and Islamic Jihad. For years Hamas had chipped away at any prestige Arafat had left with ordinary Palestinians by providing free education, medical services, and a stronger response to Israeli occupation. A new group known as the Al-Aqsa Martyrs' Brigade, drawn from Arafat's own Fatah party, also undermined the Palestinian Authority by organizing devastating suicide bombings within the Jewish state.

Despite these troubles, Arafat remained optimistic about his political future: Because of the ongoing violence against Israeli citizens, Israel would have to give in and negotiate with his Palestinian Authority. If they did, according to Arafat's logic, his waning popularity might rebound; extremists like Hamas, Islamic Jihad, and Al-Aqsa Martyrs' Brigade would lose out. But Arafat miscalculated. The waves of bloody violence did little to further peace or prop up Arafat; instead, it only plunged the region into a deeper sense of despair.

On March 27, 2002, a suicide bomber sent by Hamas blew himself up in a hotel in the city of Netanya, where Jews were holding a Passover seder. The bombing murdered twenty-nine people. "This is a trial (attempt) . . . to send a message, to all the world that we are trying to fight for our own freedom against a terrorist government in Israel led by Sharon,"[62] said a Hamas spokesman. Sharon responded to the message by delivering one of his own, called "Operation Defense Shield." Thousands of IDF forces poured into the West Bank and flattened nearly everything the Authority had built. Soldiers arrested nearly nine thousand Palestinians and killed hundreds more. In the city of Jenin, the IDF battled militants and bulldozed much of the old quarter. Jenin's large refugee camp became a particular target, a place that military officials believed was often used to plan terrorist attacks. Finally, Israeli forces entered Ramallah and destroyed Arafat's headquarters with the Authority leader still inside.

Hunkered down, cut off from both his people and the international community, Arafat appointed long-time Fatah leader Mahmoud Abbas as Authority prime minister in early 2003. But Arafat refused to cede any real power to Abbas, who quickly resigned. Arafat replaced him. The fighting slowed in 2004 when Hamas suggested it would stop the suicide attacks against the State of Israel, but no official truce was called. Surprisingly, the savage legacy of the second intifada soon led to one of the most stunning breakthroughs in Israeli-Palestinian relations ever.

Potential Breakthrough

On February 2, 2004, Sharon announced a unilateral withdrawal from the Gaza Strip. Unlike past practice, Israeli forces would not leave one area only to occupy

another. Instead, Sharon made plans for all troops to leave the territory at once. The announcement sent shock waves through both Israeli and Palestinian communities. But planning a withdrawal and carrying one out was not the same thing. Palestinians distrusted a man many of them considered, at the very least, a warmonger. Jewish Israelis feared internal conflict between those who hailed the withdrawal and those settlers determined to stay.

Meanwhile, Arafat had taken ill. In late October he was flown to Paris for medical treatment but he soon slipped into a coma and died on November 11, 2004. The controversial Palestinian leader was flown home and buried in Ramallah.

With less political baggage than Arafat, Abbas took steps to make peace with Israel. As a sign of confidence in his leadership abilities, Palestinians elected Abbas to succeed Arafat as Au-

Israeli prime minister Ariel Sharon (right) and Palestinian president Mahmoud Abbas shake hands at a meeting at Sharm el-Sheikh on February 8, 2005, after agreeing to a cease-fire.

thority president in January 2005. Less than a month later, Abbas and Sharon announced a cease-fire at the Sharm el-Sheikh summit in Egypt. Abbas promised to cease violence against Israelis. Sharon acknowledged the gesture and responded in kind: "We agreed that all Palestinians will stop all acts of violence against all Israelis everywhere, and, at the same time, Israel will cease all its military activity against all Palestinians everywhere."[63]

Over the course of the intifada, 3.4 Palestinians died for every Israeli killed. In all, 3,386 Palestinians died, of which 676 were children; 992 Israelis

Arab League Offers Peace

Formed in Cairo, Egypt, in 1945, the Arab League began with six member nations: Egypt, Syria, Lebanon, Saudi Arabia, Iraq, and Transjordan (now known as Jordan). It now includes twenty-two Arab countries. Although the league's initial goals were to create political, economic, and cultural ties between Arab nations, its early years were marked by a staunch refusal to acknowledge the State of Israel. Then, in a 2002 turnaround, Arab League member Saudi Arabia proposed an Arab Peace Initiative. With an eye toward ending the Arab-Israeli Conflict, Saudi crown prince Abdullah called for normalizing relations with Israel in exchange for Israel's withdrawal to its pre-1967 borders. The Palestinian Authority has embraced the plan, while the Israeli government's response has been mixed. Some Israeli leaders appear encouraged by the Arab League's willingness to work with them, but others remain unwilling to discuss withdrawing from the Territories and are wary of the organization's motives. More broadly, American and European leaders have cautiously embraced the initiative. In March 2009 U.S. special envoy George Mitchell announced that the Obama administration may include the Arab Peace Initiative in its future Middle East policy.

were killed, 118 of them children. Now it was officially over. Egyptian president Hosni Mubarak, who acted as an important mediator in the peace effort, offered cautious optimism that the worst was over. "The challenges today are large and deep," he said, "but the mission is not impossible. If the road is long, we today took the first step."[64]

This tenuous peace was not always echoed in other parts of the Middle East. The U.S. occupation of Iraq was now in its second year, and the fighting between militant factions and the U.S. military had grown ever fiercer. Then, just days after the Sharm el-Sheikh summit, former Lebanese prime minis-

ter Rafik Hariri was killed when his motorcade exploded in Beirut. Hariri's opposition to Syrian influence in Lebanon made him a marked man and proved that instability still reigned in Middle Eastern politics.

In Israel the violence had not ended completely either. As the Israeli cabinet voted to leave the Palestinian areas retaken during the intifada, an Islamic Jihad suicide bombing in Tel Aviv murdered five people. In response, Sharon halted all plans to leave Palestinian towns. The move proved temporary, but it kept the Israelis on their guard. Meanwhile, Great Britain organized much-needed financial aid to the

Palestinian Authority. Abbas's visit to the White House in May also bore fruit, as President George W. Bush promised $50 million in aid to the ailing government. But the biggest headlines were reserved for Israel's next major military venture, one that delighted Palestinians but infuriated Zionist factions within Israel itself.

Israel Leaves Gaza

After nearly forty years, Israel promised to make good on one portion of UN Resolution 242. Its planned withdrawal from Gaza had been in the works for many months, but as the deadline for final withdrawal approached, Sharon and his cabinet remained nervous. They hoped the thousands of settlers living in Gaza's twenty-one settlements would leave peacefully, but they also prepared for the worst, sending in tanks, jeeps, and forty thousand soldiers to remove their fellow Jewish Israelis.

"We don't know where to go,"[65] said Debbie Rosen, resident of Gaza's largest settlement, Neve Dekalim. Given two days to vacate their homes or face forcible eviction by the IDF, the settlers joined hands to form a human chain and blocked the entrance to the settlement. Computer worker Zeev Wolf and his wife drove from their own West Bank settlement to lend support. Wolf seemed dismayed by the soldiers' actions: "Instead of taking care of us," he said, "they are using force against Jews who love this country, who are trying to defend it."[66]

The soldiers themselves stood stone-faced as they were taunted and jeered by the desperate settlers. When the order

Palestinians burn U.S. and Israeli flags as they celebrate Israelis' 2005 evacuation of their settlements in Gaza.

was given, settlers who refused to budge were dragged by the soldiers into waiting cars or vans. Their commander, Brigadier General Hagai Dotan, spoke in practical terms about the high cost of providing security to a small number of pious Jews who are surrounded on three sides by Palestinians hostile to their presence. Once all of the settlers were taken away, Dotan planned to have his troops take one last look through the settlements for any dead-enders. He made his contempt for the settlers clear: "Tomorrow is cleanup day," he said, "to find the weirdos who believe the Messiah will come."[67]

For Palestinians living in Gaza, the milestone prompted a day of celebration and thanks. Many spent part of the day praying. Others took to the streets. Yet questions remained. How much autonomy would Gaza's residents truly have? How would they stimulate a long-dead economy without the help of Israel? What would the Gaza withdrawal mean for Palestinian resistance and for violent groups such as Hamas?

"If there's no Israeli occupation, there is no need for resistance," said Abu Faddak. "If they leave Gaza, we won't fight from Gaza. But if they're still in Ramallah, there will be resistance in Ramallah."[68] Faddak spoke for many Palestinians who were joyful at Israel's action in Gaza but remained unwavering in their demand for all of the Occupied Territories. The last Israeli soldiers left the Gaza Strip on September 1, 2005. Also evacuated were four West Bank settlements. Two weeks later

Sharon gave a speech at United Nations headquarters in New York. He reasserted Israel's right to Jerusalem while also acknowledging Palestinian rights. For its part, the Palestinian Authority passed a law banning parades and weapons in Gaza, but a final parade through Gaza's streets turned tragic when an accidental explosion killed twenty people.

Hamas Is Elected

The Gaza withdrawal caused far greater problems, both for the Palestinian Authority and Sharon's Likud Party. In late September Sharon won a crucial vote within his party against members opposed to withdrawal from Gaza, but Likud put the prime minister on notice that they were watching his actions very closely. Meanwhile, Palestinian factions launched rocket attacks into Israel, forcing Israel to respond. By November, facing pressure on all sides, Sharon resigned from the Likud Party and formed a new one called Kadima.

Internal struggles among Palestinian factions also made headlines. In a local election for the Palestinian parliament, Hamas won twenty-four seats. While Fatah remained in the majority, the popularity of Hamas continued to grow. And by now, fighting between Fatah and Hamas had killed three people. The groups were vying for the chance to lead Palestinians into a new age. More elections were planned for late January, but Sharon would not be there to see them. On January 4, the former general who had taken the un-

The Hamas co-founder, Palestinian Mahmoud Zahar, insisted his organization did not use terrorist tactics to halt Israeli aggression.

liamentary elections. Hamas's victory promised to pose serious challenges for the peace process. Israel viewed Hamas not as a governmental organization like Fatah or even a group of politicians with whom they could negotiate; they were terrorists, pure and simple. Olmert drew the line clearly: "Israel will not conduct any negotiation with a Palestinian government, if it includes any (members of) an armed terror organization that calls for Israel's destruction."[69] Hamas cofounder Mahmoud Zahar was equally defiant, but denied accusations of terrorism: "We are not playing terrorism or violence. We are under occupation. The Israelis are continuing their aggression against our people, killing, detention, demolition and in order to stop these processes, we run effective self defense by all means, including using guns."[70]

The stunning developments signaled the potential end of the forty-year leadership of Fatah and the PLO. Fatah's Abbas could only speak of his continued desire for peace, but it seemed fewer were willing to listen. Now in charge of the Palestinian Authority, Hamas was adamant: It still refused to recognize Israel's right to exist and said that the fight for a free Palestine would continue. Countries, including the United States, subsequently suspended financial aid payments until Hamas changed its mind. In defiance, Hamas officials smuggled cash into the West Bank and Gaza to keep the Palestinian Authority running and emergency funds to its people flowing.

precedented action on behalf of peace in the Middle East suffered a massive stroke and fell into a coma. Veteran politician and fellow Kadima member Ehud Olmert took his place.

Only days later, Israel and the world received another shock when Hamas won 76 out of 132 seats in the new par-

Militarily, Hamas, Islamic Jihad, and other factions continued firing Qassam rockets into Israel from locations in the Gaza Strip. In March forty rockets rained down on the southwestern city of Sderot. Again, the IDF responded by shelling targets on Gaza. By June Israeli forces had invaded Gaza in an effort to halt the attack and retrieve a kidnapped soldier.

War with Hezbollah

In July Israel found itself attacked on another front. In the early morning hours, Hezbollah launched rocket attacks from southern Lebanon into northern Israel. Hezbollah used the attack as a decoy while ground forces moved into Israel and attacked troops stationed near the city of Zar'it. Three Israeli soldiers were killed, two injured, and two kidnapped. Hezbollah leader Hassan Nasrallah planned to trade the captured soldiers for his own fighters.

Outraged by Hezbollah's actions, Olmert promised swift retaliation, calling the attacks an act of war. IDF chief of staff Dan Halutz was even more blunt. "If the soldiers are not returned, we will turn Lebanon's clock back 20 years,"[71] he said.

Following through on that promise, the Israeli air force bombarded locations in Beirut, including the Rafiq Hariri Airport, along with bridges, tunnels, and other Lebanese infrastructure. Hospitals, markets, schools, and mosques were also destroyed, killing scores of Lebanese men, women, and children. It became clear to most observers that aside from destroying Hezbollah's ability to attack, Israel

The head of Lebanon's Shiite Muslim movement, Hezbollah, Sheikh Hassan Nasrallah led the July 2006 assault on northern Israel.

wanted to convince Lebanese civilians to overthrow Hezbollah leadership. It did not work. Instead Hezbollah launched even more ferocious rocket attacks into cities in northern Israel, shattering the lives of Israelis who lived there.

Leaders in the international community saw the carnage and recognized Israel's right to defend itself. For the most part, though, they refused to criticize the Jewish state's war tactics. Instead, the G-8, comprised of the world's most industrialized nations, released a statement condemning Hezbollah alone: "These extremist elements and those that support them cannot be allowed to plunge the Middle East into chaos and provoke a wider conflict. The extremists must immediately halt their attacks."[72] The conflict did end after thirty-four days. Fourteen hundred Lebanese civilians died, as did forty-three Israeli civilians.

Articles released later in the *Asia Times* and other publications around the world suggested that American president George W. Bush's administration had helped the Israelis plan the assault on Hezbollah. These reports implied that the Americans were planning their own attack in the region against the nuclear facilities of Iran, and the Hezbollah action served as a prelude.

War in Gaza and Netanyahu's Return

A UN-sponsored cease-fire in Lebanon changed little in Gaza. Hamas and others continued their own rocket assault in southwestern Israel. For eight years Hamas had fired into the Jewish state from the strip, terrorizing border towns. By December 2008 Olmert decided on a stronger response. In what experts called the most lethal assaults on Palestinian areas since 1967, Operation Solid Lead killed nearly four hundred Hamas and Islamic Jihad fighters in the first few days of fighting. On January 4, 2009, Israel ordered ground troops into Gaza to root out its fighters.

Hamas, supplied and trained by Iran and Hezbollah, struggled to hold its own against a far superior military force by planting booby traps and roadside bombs. "Urban warfare is the most difficult battlefield, where Hamas and Islamic Jihad have a relative advantage, with local knowledge and prepared positions,"[73] says military expert Jonathan Fighel.

For its part, the IDF and special commando units went all out to destroy its enemy. "We are very violent," says one commander. "We do not balk at any means to protect the lives of our soldiers."[74] During the violence, water lines were cut, leaving thousands of Palestinians in a dire situation. But street-to-street fighting continued until January 18, when both sides announced a cease-fire. Israel withdrew three days later.

Less than a month later, Israeli elections gave Likud a boost. Soon after, Netanyahu, who again campaigned on a policy of getting tough with the Palestinians, formed a coalition government and became Israel's new prime minister. In a tense meeting with American president Barack Obama in May, he showed little willingness to compromise on key disputes between Israelis and Palestinians, especially the issue of settlements.

In June 2009 Netanyahu gave a major speech at Bar-Ilan University, calling for a complete disarmament in any proposed Palestinian state. He also refused calls to dismantle Jewish settlements in the West Bank. "We will not build new settlements," he said. "But it is not fair not to provide a solution to natural growth."[75]

Time for Action?

Netanyahu's comments suggest that peace can wait. In reality, time is running out for the State of Israel. In less than a decade there will be more Palestinians than Jewish Israelis in Israel, Gaza, and the West Bank. While the Israelis could try evicting Palestinians from the West Bank, they might also be forced to rule the majority Palestinians in an apartheid-like system in which the Palestinians would have no vote and few rights. Least likely of all for Israel would be to allow Palestinians the vote. In that case, Jewish politicians would be voted out of office and Israel would cease to be a Jewish nation. "Time is no longer on the side of those who favor two states,"[76] says journalist Daoud Kuttab.

For its part, Hamas has outwardly declared a desire to make peace with the Israelis. Bent on Israel's destruction for twenty years, Hamas claims to want to change the political equation in the Middle East. "You will find not just Hamas, but also the Palestinian people and all the Arabs keen on making real peace," says Hamas chief Khaled Mashaal, "one based on restoring rights and free of occupation."[77]

Nabil Abu Rdeneh, an aide to Abbas, sees the road to peace another way. First, the Palestinians must accept the concept known as the two-state solution —two nations, Israel and Palestine, existing side-by-side in relative peace. They must also agree to recognize the rule of law. "To build our country and our state," says Rdeneh, "we need to have one authority, one gun, one law."[78]

Casting a shadow over any further negotiations between the Israelis and Palestinians is the threat posed by Iran, which is believed to be developing nuclear weapons. In the recent past, Iranian president Mahmoud Ahmadinejad has called the Holocaust a hoax and said that Israel should be destroyed.

A poll taken in May 2009 reports that 66 percent of Israelis support a strike on Iran's nuclear facilities as a way of protecting themselves and their country. "There is a national consensus in Israel," writes scholar Caroline B. Glick, "that preventing Iran from acquiring nuclear weapons is the most important and urgent national security challenge facing the country."[79]

By late 2009 Israel had expressed a clear willingness to find a two-state solution by leaving the Gaza Strip and halting new West Bank construction. Many of their Arab neighbors such as Saudi Arabia, Jordan, and Syria appeared more ready than ever to recog-

A Palestinian boy wearing army-style fatigues takes part in a 2009 protest outside the United Nations headquarters in Beirut. Tension between Palestinians and Israelis still remains high.

nize the existence of the Israeli state and work to resolve the age-old regional conflict. But Iran's nuclear ambitions and Israel's refusal to dismantle West Bank settlements promises to postpone any permanent solution and complicate negotiations with the Palestinians for the foreseeable future.

Epilogue

Endless War or Hopeful Future?

Since Israel's withdrawal from Gaza in 2005, little has changed for the 1.5 million Palestinians who live there. "Right after the war, everybody came—journalists, foreign governments and charities promising to help," says Hashem Dardona. "Now, nobody comes."[80] Dozens of Palestinians remain stranded in rickety tents or broken buildings; Israel has banned the importing of construction materials. But Gaza residents can no longer blame Israel for all of their problems. Hamas took over the strip of land more than two years ago and has done little to make life better for the suffering masses. If anything, Hamas has made the strip more vulnerable. Crumbling infrastructure and desperate leadership leave open the possibility that a nuclear-armed Iran could use the area to launch rocket attacks against Israel. Such attacks would meet with a swift and brutal response by Israeli forces

and likely kill thousands of Palestinian civilians.

As for the joining of Gaza and the West Bank to form a Palestinian state, the distance between the areas makes this option less and less likely. The bleak situation leads many Palestinians in dark directions. "The people of Gaza are depressed, and depressed people turn to myth and fantasy, meaning religion and drugs," says Jawdat Khoudary, a building contractor. "This kind of a prison feeds extremism."[81]

One program in Gaza encourages teens to turn away from violence and to express themselves—their frustration, their pain—through art. Twenty-year-old Farah Abu Qasem is a volunteer with the program and cannot help but notice the bleak art that the students often produce. "They seem only to choose black and to draw things like tanks," she says. "And when we ask them to draw something that represents the future, they leave the paper blank."[82]

One American organization is attempting to fill that blank page for Jews. The Jewish Dialogue Group, started in Philadelphia in 2001, fosters discussion about the Israeli-Palestinian conflict with Jews of all persuasions, be they Orthodox, secular, or somewhere in between.

Rebecca Ennen first attended a session in 2006, only months after her first trip to Israel. "I liked the idea of people talking out differences in a respectful way," she says. "I wanted to learn to be less combative, more able to talk with

Young Arab girls join members of Seeds of Peace for a "Beyond the Borders" conference.

people I don't agree with."[83] That first session led to Rebecca volunteering with the group and eventually leading dialogues. Today, she works as a program assistant and writer. Her latest project is helping to transcribe the opinions of some of the Jews who attend the sessions and turn them into a book. "I think it's great for Jews to talk to each other about the conflict. If we can't talk to each other respectfully and with compassion, how can we expect to hear or speak with Palestinians?"[84]

Seeds of Peace, another group, brings together young people whose nations are in conflict. Children and teens from a variety of countries—India, Pakistan, Jordan, Somalia—attend camp and work with each other in a series of team-building exercises. They also room together to develop mutual understanding and respect. Started in 1993 soon after the Oslo Peace Accords, Israeli, Palestinian, and Egyptian kids were the first campers. By working and living together they learned they were not so different after all. The future of the Middle East may lie in their hands. "Governments negotiate treaties," reads a camp sign. "Peace is made by people."[85]

Peace is possible, as the people of Northern Ireland recently discovered when Protestant and Catholic militias laid down their arms in the long-standing conflict between them. But the history of the Israeli-Palestinian conflict suggests that if peace does someday arrive, reaching it will be a painstaking and arduous process full of difficult sacrifices.

Notes

Introduction: Decades of Conflict

1. Quoted in Nina Burleigh, "Israeli Settlers Versus the Palestinians," *Time*, July 27, 2009. www.time.com/time/magazine/article/0,9171,1910975,00. html?artId= 1910975?contType=article ?chn=us.

2. Quoted in Burleigh, "Israeli Settlers Versus the Palestinians."

3. Quoted in Burleigh, "Israeli Settlers Versus the Palestinians."

Chapter One: Origins of the Conflict

4. Mark Twain, *The Innocents Abroad*. New York: Library of America, 1984, p. 485.

5. Quoted in Joan Acocella, "Betrayal," *New Yorker*, August 3, 2009, p. 71.

6. Quoted in Mark A. Tessler, *A History of the Israeli-Palestinian Conflict*. Bloomington: Indiana University Press, 1994, p. 136.

7. Benny Morris, *1948: The First Arab-Israeli War*. New Haven, CT: Yale University Press, 2008, p. 4.

8. Morris, *1948: The First Arab-Israeli War*, p. 5.

9. Quoted in Mehran Kamrava, *The Modern Middle East*. Berkeley: University of California Press, 2005, p. 73.

10. Quoted in Walter Laqueur, *A History of Zionism*. London: I.B. Tauris, 2003, p. 239.

11. Quoted in "The Palestine Mandate," *The Avalon Project: Documents in Law, History and Diplomacy*, 2008. http://avalon.law.yale.edu/20th_century/palmanda.asp.

12. Quoted in Rashid Khalidi, "The Palestinians and 1948," *The War for Palestine*, eds. Eugene L. Rogan and Avi Shlaim. Cambridge, UK: Cambridge University Press, 2007, p. 29.

13. Quoted in Morris, *1948: The First Arab-Israeli War*, p. 3.

14. Quoted in *Israel: Birth of a Nation*, History Channel, 1997.

15. Quoted in *Israel: A Nation Is Born*, Home Vision Entertainment, 1997.

16. Quoted in *Israel: A Nation Is Born*.

17. Quoted in *Israel: Birth of a Nation*.

18. Quoted in *Israel: Birth of a Nation*.

19. David Ben-Gurion, *Memoirs*. New York: World, 1970, p. 26.

Chapter Two: Israel and Its Neighbors

20. Quoted in Efraim Karsh, *Islamic Imperialism*. New Haven, CT: Yale University Press, 2007, p. 144.

21. Quoted in John B. Quigley, *Palestine and Israel*. Durham, NC: Duke University Press, 1990, p. 64.

22. Helena Lindholm Schulz, *The Palestinian Diaspora*. New York: Routledge, 2003, p. 24.

23. Morris, *1948: The First Arab-Israeli War*, p. 420.

24. Quoted in Benny Morris, *Israel's Border Wars, 1949–1956*. New York: Oxford University Press, 1997, p. 285.

25. Quoted in Morris, *Israel's Border Wars, 1949–1956*, p. 286.

26. Michael B. Oren, *Six Days of War: June 1967 and the Making of the Modern Middle East*. New York: Oxford University Press, 2002, p. 12.

27. Quoted in Oren, *Six Days of War*, p. 19.

28. Quoted in Oren, *Six Days of War*, p. 26.

29. Quoted in Michael E. Staub, *Torn at the Roots: The Crisis of Jewish Liberalism in Postwar America*. New York: Columbia University Press, 2004, p. 128.

30. Quoted in Staub, *Torn at the Roots*, p. 129.

31. William Scott Green and Jed Silverstein, "The Doctrine of the Messiah," *The Blackwell Companion to Judaism*, eds. Jacob Neusner and Alan Avery-Peck. Hoboken, NJ: Wiley, 2003, p. 262.

32. Quoted in Gershom Gorenberg, *The Accidental Empire: Israel and the Birth of the Settlements, 1967–1977*. New York: Macmillan, 2007, p. 151.

33. Avi Shlaim, *The Iron Wall: Israel and the Arab World*. New York: W.W. Norton & Co., 2001, p. 309.

34. Quoted in Mehran Kamrava, *The Modern Middle East*. Berkeley: University of California Press, 2005, p. 127.

Chapter Three: Palestinians Find a Voice

35. Baruch Kimmerling, *The PLO and Israel*, eds. Avraham Sela and Moshe Maoz. New York: Palgrave Macmillan, 1997, p. 226.

36. Quoted in *One Day in September*, directed by Kevin McDonald, Sony Pictures Classics, 1999.

37. Quoted in Simon Reeve, *One Day in September*. New York: Arcade, 2000, p. 65.

38. Quoted in *One Day in September*, directed by Kevin McDonald.

39. Quoted in Itamar Rabinovich, Jehuda Reinharz, eds., *Israel in the Middle East*. Boston: Brandeis, 2007, p. 365

40. Aaron Mannes, *Profiles in Terror: A Guide to Middle East Terrorist Organizations*. Lanham, MD: Rowman & Littlefield, p. 273.

41. David W. Lesch, *The New Lion of Damascus: Bashar al-Asad and Modern Syria*. New Haven, CT: Yale University Press, 2005, p. 27.

42. Thomas L. Friedman, *From Beirut to Jerusalem*. New York: Macmillan, 1991, p. 126.

43. Quoted in Alan Raymond and Susan Raymond, *Children in War*. New York: TV Books, 2000, p. 52.

44. Quoted in Raymond and Raymond, *Children in War*, p. 54.

Chapter Four: A Chance for Peace and a Return to Violence

45. Myron J. Aronoff, *The Intifada*, ed. Robert Owen Freedman. Gainesville:

University Press of Florida, 1991, p. 336.

46. William B. Quandt, *Peace Process: American Diplomacy and the Arab-Israeli Conflict Since 1967*. Berkeley: University of California Press, 2005, p. 313.

47. Quoted in William D. Hart, *Edward Said and the Religious Effects of Culture*. Cambridge, England: Cambridge University Press, 2000, p. 148.

48. Quoted in Raymond and Raymond, *Children in War*, p. 61.

49. Quoted in Malise Ruthven, *Islam in the World*. New York: Oxford University Press, 2006, p. 415.

50. Quoted in Ehud Sprinzak, *Brother Against Brother: Violence and Extremism in Israeli Politics from Altalena to the Rabin Assassination*. New York: Simon & Schuster, 1999, p. 259.

51. Quoted in Raymond and Raymond, *Children in War*, p. 67.

52. Quoted in Sprinzak, *Brother Against Brother*, p. 248.

53. Quoted in Steven Bayme, *Jewish Arguments and Counterarguments: Essays and Addresses*. Jersey City, NJ: KTAV, 2002, p. 395.

54. Bayme, *Jewish Arguments and Counterarguments*, p. 395.

55. Quoted in Raymond and Raymond, *Children in War*, p. 64.

56. Quoted in Gorenberg, *The Accidental Empire*, pp. 371–72.

57. Quoted in Amnon Lipkin-Shahak, *The Camp David Summit—What Went Wrong?* eds. Shimon Shamir and Bruce Maddy-Weitzman. East Sussex, UK: Sussex Academic Press, 2005, p. 43.

58. Lipkin-Shahak, *The Camp David Summit—What Went Wrong?* p. 47.

Chapter Five: The Road Forward

59. Tony Karon, "Sharon Trounces Barak," *Time*, February 6, 2001. www.time.com/time/world/article/0,8599,98229,00.html.

60. Quoted in John J. Mearsheimer and Stephen M. Walt, *The Israel Lobby and U.S. Foreign Policy*. New York: Macmillan, p. 100.

61. Quoted in Mearsheimer and Walt, *The Israel Lobby and U.S. Foreign Policy*, p. 101.

62. Quoted in CNN, "'Passover Massacre' at Israeli Hotel Kills 19," March 27, 2002. http://archives.cnn.com/2002/WORLD/meast/03/27/mideast.

63. Quoted in Jaime Holguin, "'New Opportunity for Peace,'" *CBS News*, February 8, 2005. www.cbsnews.com/stories/2005/02/08/world/main672508.shtml.

64. Quoted in Holguin, "'New Opportunity for Peace.'"

65. Quoted in *BBC News*, "Settlers Protest at Gaza Pullout," August 15, 2005. http://news.bbc.co.uk/2/hi/middle_east/4150028.stm.

66. Quoted in Greg Myre, "Israeli Troops Drag Pro-Settler Squatters from Stronghold," *New York Times*, July 1, 2005. www.nytimes.com/2005/07/01/international/middleeast/01mideast.html?ex=1277870400&en=439354c042028a45&ei=5090&partner=rssuserland&emc=rss.

67. Quoted in Steven Erlanger, "Last Settlers Leave Gaza Quietly, Ending a 40-Year Era," *New York Times*, August 23, 2005. www.nytimes.com /2005/08/23/international/middle east/23gaza.html.

68. Quoted in Ilene R. Prusher, "As Israel Leaves Gaza, Will Militants Lay Down Their Guns?" *Christian Science Monitor*, September 9, 2005. www.csmonitor.com/2005/0909/p 07s01-wome.html.

69. Quoted in *BBC News*, "Hamas Sweeps to Election Victory," January 26, 2006. http://news.bbc.co.uk /2/hi/middle_east/4650788.stm.

70. Quoted in *BBC News*, "Hamas Sweeps to Election Victory."

71. Quoted in Antony Loewenstein, *My Israel Question*. Melbourne, Australia: Carlton, Vic., 2007, p. xiv.

72. Quoted in Associated Press, "Deaths Rise as Israel, Hezbollah Trade Attacks," *MSNBC*, July 17, 2006.

73. Quoted in Steven Erlanger, "A Gaza War Full of Traps and Trickery," *New York Times*, January 10, 2009. www.nytimes.com/2009/01/11/ world/middleeast/11hamas.html.

74. Quoted in Andrew Lee Butters, "Fighting the Media War in Gaza," *Time*, January 14, 2009. http://www .time.com/time/world/article/0,85 99,1871487,00.html.

75. Quoted in Amy Teibel, "Netanyahu Defies U.S. on Israeli Settlements," *Philadelphia Inquirer*, May 25, 2009, p. A3.

76. Daoud Kuttab, "Israel Must Leave Palestinian Lands," *Philadelphia Inquirer*, May 17, 2009, C1.

77. Quoted in Karin Laub (Associated Press), "Hamas Leaders Have Begun Outreach Efforts with West," *Philadelphia Inquirer*, May 19, 2009, p. A6.

78. Quoted in Ali Daraghmeh, "6 Dead in West Bank Clash," *Philadelphia Inquirer*, June 1, 2009, p. A3.

79. Caroline B. Glick, "Washington Has Abandoned Its Obligations," *Philadelphia Inquirer*, May 17, 2009, p. C1.

Epilogue: Endless War or Hopeful Future?

80. Quoted in Ethan Bronner, "Misery Hangs Over Gaza Despite Pledges of Help," *New York Times*, May 28, 2009. www.nytimes.com/2009/05/ 29/world/middleeast/29gaza.html ?hp.

81. Quoted in Bronner, "Misery Hangs Over Gaza Despite Pledges of Help."

82. Quoted in Bronner, "Misery Hangs Over Gaza Despite Pledges of Help."

83. Rebecca Ennen, interview by author, July 13, 2009.

84. Ennen, interview.

85. Quoted in Senator Susan Collins, "Sowing the Seeds of Peace," *Magic City Morning Star*, July 7, 2006. www.magic-city-news.com/Susan_ Collins_25/Sowing_the_Seeds_of_ Peace_62426242.shtml.

Glossary

diaspora: Any group migration or flight from a country or region.

extremism: To go to extremes, especially in politics.

Fatah: Palestinian political party founded in the 1950s.

fedayeen: Members of an Arab commando group.

Haganah: Early Jewish military force in British-controlled Palestine.

Hamas: Militant Palestinian organization founded in 1987.

Histadrut: Early Zionist labor union.

Holocaust: Murder of six million Jews by the Nazis during World War II.

Irgun: A Jewish paramilitary group created as an offshoot of Haganah.

Knesset: State of Israel's parliament.

Labor Party: Center-left Israeli political party.

Likud Party: Center-right Israeli political party.

Mossad: Israel's secretive intelligence agency.

Nazi Party: German national socialist political organization founded by Adolf Hitler.

Palestine Liberation Organization: Political and paramilitary organization that supports a two-state solution in the Middle East.

scapegoat: Person or group made to bear the blame for others or to suffer in their place.

Shin Bet: Israel's domestic security agency.

Temple Mount: Religious site in Jerusalem, holy to both Jews and Muslims.

terrorist: Person who terrorizes or frightens others, usually for political purposes.

Yishuv: Hebrew term referring to the community of Jews living in the Holy Land before the State of Israel came into being.

Zionism: Global Jewish movement that resulted in the establishment and development of the State of Israel.

For Further Reading

Books

Benny Morris, *1948: A History of the First Arab-Israeli War*. New Haven, CT: Yale University Press, 2008. This skillfully researched work by one of Israel's best-known historians may be the definitive account of how the state of Israel came into being and the unrest that resulted among the Arab nations of the Middle East.

Alan Raymond and Susan Raymond, *Children in War*. New York: TV Books, 2000. Consisting primarily of interviews with children who have lived through the horror of war, this moving book is a companion to an HBO documentary of the same name. The authors talk to young people all over the world, including Israel, Rwanda, and Northern Ireland.

David Rubinger, *Israel Through My Lens*. New York: Abbeville, 2008. Veteran photographer and Austrian émigré to Israel, Rubinger fought in the first Arab-Israeli war and then made a career as a photojournalist. For sixty years, Rubinger has captured Israeli life and history. His book is a testament to the journey of his people.

Raja Shehadeh, *Palestinian Walks: Forays into a Vanishing Landscape*. New York: Scribner, 2008. The author, a Palestinian lawyer and human rights activist, writes of his grief and anger over Is-raeli occupation. He also voices his frustration with Palestinian leaders and holds out little hope for peace. Still, his book provides an insider's view of life in the West Bank.

Mark Tessler, *A History of the Israeli-Palestinian Conflict*. Bloomington: Indiana University Press, 2009. For an exhaustive history of the conflict, try Tessler's highly respected tome. The author works for complete objectivity, taking no sides and presenting the facts as best he can. No Middle Eastern stone is left unturned in this more than thousand-page text.

Periodicals

Ali Daraghmeh, "6 Dead in West Bank Clash," *Philadelphia Inquirer*, June 1, 2009.

John Heilprin, "U.N. Report Faults Israel in Gaza Attacks," *Philadelphia Inquirer*, May 6, 2009.

Amy Teibel, "Netanyahu Defies U.S. on Israeli Settlements," *Philadelphia Inquirer*, May 25, 2009.

Web Sites

Al Haq (www.alhaq.org). Based in Ramallah in the West Bank, Al Haq is a Palestinian human rights organization that seeks to document violation of the rights of Palestinians and Israelis. The group's Web site includes links to international law policies on human rights and a list of the latest publications on the conflict.

B'Tselem (www.btselem.org/English/index.asp). Also known as the Israeli Information Center for Human Rights, this organization, according to its Web site, "endeavors to document and educate the Israeli public and policymakers about human rights violations in the Occupied Territories, combat the phenomenon of denial prevalent among the Israeli public, and help create a human rights culture in Israel."

Gush-Shalom (http://zope.gush-shalom.org/index_en.html). Self-described "hard core of the Israeli peace movement," Gush-Shalom's Web site contains left-leaning opinion columns on the conflict and photo galleries of recent peace demonstrations across the globe.

Human Rights Watch, Middle East/North Africa (www.hrw.org/en/middle-east/n-africa). For the latest on how the Middle East conflict affects the lives of ordinary Palestinians and Israelis, check out this watchdog's site. According to its Web site, Human Rights Watch works to "give voice to the oppressed and hold oppressors accountable for their crimes."

Jewish Dialogue Group (http://jewishdialogue.org). Formed in 2001, this Philadelphia-based organization attempts to foster constructive dialogue within Jewish communities about the Israeli-Palestinian conflict. The group's Web site includes information about upcoming meetings in the United States and Israel, as well as a guidebook that can be used by those interested in facilitating a workshop about the issue.

Middle East Policy Council (www.mepc.org/main/main.asp). This independent, nonprofit group provides a forum for discussions related to the Middle East by publishing the quarterly journal *Middle East Policy* and holding frequent workshops for students of all ages.

ProCon.org (http://israelipalestinian.procon.org/viewtopic.asp). Clear and concise, ProCon lays out the issues in the Israeli-Palestinian conflict in a way that cuts to the very core of the dispute. A handy top ten includes topics such as "Hamas and the Peace Process," "Two-State Solution," and "Significance of Jerusalem to Jews and Muslims."

Surfing for Peace (www.surfing4peace.org). Founded in 2007 by Jewish American surfer Dorian "Doc" Paskowitz, Surfing for Peace, according to its Web site, "aims to bridge cultural and political barriers between surfers in the Middle East." The organization supplies Gaza athletes with surfboards so they can catch the "radical" Mediterranean waves and hosts fundraising events to support cross-cultural understanding.

Index

Picture Credits

About the Author

David Robson is the recipient of two playwriting fellowships from the Delaware Division of the Arts; his plays have been performed across the country and abroad. He is also the author of several Lucent titles for young adults, including *The Murder of Emmett Till*, *Auschwitz*, and *The Black Arts Movement*. David holds an MFA degree from Goddard College, an MS from Saint Joseph's University, and a BA from Temple University. He lives with his family in Wilmington, Delaware.